Upholstery:

refinishing and restyling

Benjamin C. Luna
Compton High School
Compton, California

AMERICAN TECHNICAL SOCIETY, CHICAGO 60637

ISBNO-8269-4545-7

Printed in the United States of America

PREFACE

Upholstery: Refinishing and Restyling is the answer to many requests from students who kept asking for written material on the lectures and sketches used in my classes.

There is no one "best way" but in my 8 years of teaching and more than 18 years of work in the trade I developed methods that were economical, produced quality work, and that assured personal and customer satisfaction.

It is easier to present these methods, and also for the student to understand, if sketches and diagrams are used. So drawings have been used to bring out the instructions in the book as I have done at the blackboard in my classes.

The diagrams and illustrations cover only two or three different styles of chairs, sofas, and a bed divan. To include instructions on the dozens of styles of chairs and sofas would be an incredible task and, frankly, most of the material would be repetitious as you would find, as I did, that once the basic methods were learned on one style that the other styles were really very little different. I have covered the subject so that all the fundamental knowledge and information is available to the reader. The illustrations are from own drawings.

Writing the book has been a challenge. It has taken several years to compile and put down the experiences gained in many years of working in upholstery and in teaching the subject as both a vocation and a hobby. I have been encouraged by educators and former students, who have seen all or part of the manuscript. They regard it as meeting the need for a book geared to all types of students. Questions have been included to assist in understanding the text.

The cooperation of furniture manufacturers, equipment makers and suppliers, upholsterer unions, technical schools, and individuals has made this book possible. Their assistance is acknowledged and gratefully appreciated. My deepest gratitude goes to the many people who have worked to transform the manuscript into type.

BENJAMIN C. LUNA

Contents

Learning to Upholster

Chapter 1

INTRODUCTION

In learning to upholster you will need to know the terms the trade uses and also the various kinds of special tools and supplies.

You will also learn to have patience if you succeed. Almost all operations in upholstering involve skills that you will need to develop. That means you will repeat some operations over and over until you master the fine points.

The object of the first project is to show you the structure of furniture and to teach you the names of the various parts, how they are put together, the tools used, and the materials. So get an upholstered chair that needs recovering and be prepared to reupholster it from top to bottom.

A chair is chosen for the simple reason that it is basically no different to upholster than a sofa. It is easier to handle and has all the parts that you encounter in furniture work. Be careful to select a chair that will not be missed, otherwise there may be family pressure to finish it in a hurry. On your first project you will need extra time to develop new skills and learn new procedures. You must become skillful in handling unfamiliar supplies and in using new tools.

ORDER OF OPERATIONS

In upholstering there is a definite order of operations. One must be done before another can be started. The inside part of the chair is finished first and the upholsterers call this work *insiding*. The outside part of the chair is finished last and is called *outsiding*. In some large

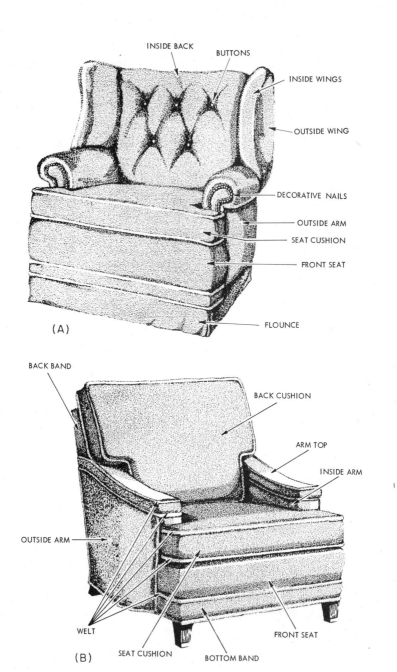

INSIDE BACK
BUTTONS
INSIDE WINGS
OUTSIDE WING
DECORATIVE NAILS
OUTSIDE ARM
SEAT CUSHION
FRONT SEAT
FLOUNCE
(A)

BACK BAND
BACK CUSHION
ARM TOP
INSIDE ARM
OUTSIDE ARM
WELT
SEAT CUSHION
BOTTOM BAND
FRONT SEAT
(B)

Fig. 1-1. The parts of upholstered chairs, A-wing style, B-Lawson style.

shops there are individuals who do nothing but insiding while others work only on outsiding. In most shops the workman must be familiar with both.

As you work on your chair you will learn that the order of operations is necessary to give a finished chair. Some operations serve as a basis for others. Some are a foundation for the final work. Others serve to complete or finish some of the earlier work.

To be able to perform the operations you must learn the names of the various parts and areas that you will work with. The inside work or order of insiding goes (1) the seat deck and front seat, (2) the bottom band, (3) the inside arms, (4) the inside wings, and (5) the inside back and back band. Some styles will not have some of these areas and they are omitted but the order of the others remains the same.

In applying the outsiding the order is slightly different. It is (1) the outside wings, (2) the outside arms, (3) the outside back, (4) the panels, (5) the flounce, and (6) the cambric.

While some of these, such as the flounce and the wings, may not be used on some styles of furniture the order of operations remains the same with the unused parts omitted. Study Fig. 1–1 until you are familiar with the parts.

You will notice that there are certain items shown on the chairs that are not listed in the order of operations. These are additional terms that you should learn and their meanings. They will be covered in detail when their use in reupholstering the chair is needed.

TOOLS AND SUPPLIES

In upholstering you need some special tools. These will be shown and their use explained at the place where they will first be used. You will use standard tools in some cases such as hand saws, drill and bits, clamps, and a square.

A heavy-duty sewing machine, a button machine, and a cushion stuffer are machines that are used in shops and are found in almost all schools. They speed up the work. The person who is doing upholstering as a hobby or is getting started may not have access to these machines. In these cases you can improvise some of them such as a cushion stuffer by using cardboard or sheet metal to make a telescoping case that will do the work. A home type sewing machine can be used for sewing muslin, welting, and materials that are thin and have little strain on the seams. For the fabric cover the home machine will not do a very satisfactory job. Heavy thread is needed and home sewing machines do not have the size or power to handle the heavy thread especially when sewing through several thicknesses of heavy fabric.

If it is impossible to borrow or use a professional sewing machine you might have your tailor or laundry sew the seams on the cover. If no sewing machines are available you can, as a last resort, use a home type machine. Be sure to use the heaviest thread and the largest stitch setting that the machine will handle. Where the material is several layers thick turn the machine slowly by hand to avoid breaking the thread or needle. Remember that such seams are much more likely to pull out and give trouble than if done on a professional machine.

Buttons are easily covered with a button machine. Without a machine you can buy covered buttons in matching or contrasting colors to your fabric. Upholstery supply houses may be able to suggest firms that would cover buttons for you.

Many items can only be obtained from a company that specializes in upholstery supplies. It would be helpful to contact such a firm before you start your upholstery. Then you will know what is available or what is being used commercially. Different styles of furniture require somewhat different materials. These will be explained where they are needed.

Upholstery deals only with furniture that is covered in cloth, leather, or plastic and that has soft backs and seats, padded arms, and cushions. Overstuffed is a name frequently applied to upholstered items.

Some of the methods and skills used in upholstering furniture are applied to other items such as padded headboards for beds, padded doors and walls, and pillows. Many kinds of kitchen, occasional, or office furniture employ some of the materials and techniques used in upholstering. A person who has learned the skills of upholstering will have no difficulty in working on all kinds of padded furniture and many other objects such as boats and cars.

SAFE WORK PRACTICES

Upholstering is all hand work. The tools used are fairly simple and easily handled. There is no complex machinery or hazardous tools used except in factories and special training is needed to operate them.

However, in dealing with new materials there are certain safety measures that may prevent injuries. These are, for the most part, general measures that should be observed as a regular part of the work.

1. Hold and use tools correctly. The correct way is explained when necessary.

2. Keep work area clean. Many tacks are used and some will be sure to get on the floor. Wear shoes with thick or tough soles, keep the floor swept clean, avoid kneeling, sitting, or putting the hands on the floor without making sure first that there are no tacks there.

3. Furniture may be heavy. Lift carefully by keeping the back straight and using the knees to do the lifting. Get help in handling large or heavy items. Be sure that the furniture is firmly placed so that it will not fall from the work table or trestle. A padded edge around the work table or trestle will protect the furniture and prevent the furniture and tools from sliding off.

4. Springs have a tendency to snap. Keep face and other parts of body away from springs when working with them.

5. Electric drills and sewing machines will be used. Be sure these

are properly connected and grounded. Observe the safety rules that are supplied with them.

6. Needles are common hazards. Upholstery needles are large and sharp. Keep them in a definite place and return ones that are not in use. Do not play with them. Discard any that become bent, broken, or dull.

7. Old frames may have rough places or splinters. Sand these so that they are smooth as you will be working with them regularly. Remove old tacks and nails.

8. Follow directions when using bleaches and other chemicals in refinishing wood surfaces. Safety precautions appear on the containers and should be followed explicitly.

9. Place all tools and supplies on table or trestle. Keep floor free of anything that might cause tripping or slipping.

10. Do not wear loose clothing that could get in the way or catch on objects.

11. Old tacks, staples, springs, and other waste material should be placed in a waste container as soon as possible. The waste container needs to have a tight bottom and sides to prevent spilling tacks or other small pieces of metal.

SHOP SET-UP

The proper teaching of upholstery or of doing the work needs an adequate workshop. There should be ample room so that each piece of furniture can be worked on from all sides without difficulty. Light must be good. Some operations need careful measuring, folding, and fastening so the lighting must be bright enough to enable the work to be done without eyestrain. Ventilation should be provided. Special exhaust fans may be needed where frame refinishing is being done to remove wood dust and fumes from paint and varnish remover, stain, bleaches, and other materials that get into the air and might cause dust and health problems.

The minimum needs for a small shop would include a long table for layout and cutting that is about five by eight feet, two trestles or a large work table for each piece of furniture that is being upholstered, a small table or bench space to hold supplies and tools for each student.

Each student will need his own selection of special hand tools which includes a ripping chisel, webbing stretcher, assorted needles, and magnetic tack hammer. These can be obtained in kits.

General equipment that should be available includes a hand drill (preferably electric) and bits, screwdrivers, hand saws, gluing clamps, rulers and tape measures, and upholsterer's shears.

Special equipment for upholstering includes a heavy duty sewing machine, a cushion stuffer, and a button covering machine. There are several models of each of these.

In addition to the basic items there are many special tools that are used where alternate methods or materials are employed. Among these are power staplers, spring clip clinchers, edge wire clip pliers, metal webbing stretchers, and special chisels and pliers for removing staples and nails.

The use of the tools and equipment is explained in the text where each is first used.

QUESTIONS FOR STUDY

1. What is insiding?
2. Why is there a definite order in upholstering work?
3. Which part of a chair is finished first?
4. Name and describe the location of seven parts of a chair.
5. List four safety practices and give the reason for each.
6. Where else can a knowledge of upholstering furniture be applied?
7. What are the objections to home sewing machines?
8. List the minimum requirements for a small shop.

Chapter 2

Preparing the Frame

New frames for upholstered furniture are used almost entirely in factories. Most of the work done in upholstery shops is on old frames. While technically this might be called reupholstering there is absolutely no difference in the operations whether the frame is new or old. The one difference that does come in is that the upholsterer may have to prepare the frame rather than having it come from a furniture maker.

In order to obtain a frame to work with it is necessary for the upholsterer to prepare the frame. This means that the old materials must be removed, the frame inspected for any problems that might arise, and put in condition for the new upholstering to be applied.

STRIPPING THE FRAME

You first must remove the old material from the furniture so that you can have the frame to work on. This is called stripping. However, in removing the old covering and padding you can learn a great deal about how the furniture was upholstered and also where any problems have developed.

To start you get the furniture up where you can work on it. You will need a work bench or table, sawhorses, or upholsterer's trestles. The trestles are sawhorses with wide tops and padded edges around them. Fig 2–1. You can make one by nailing an 8-inch board on a sawhorse about 30 inches high and then tacking a small roll of burlap around the edges to keep the furniture from getting scratched or sliding off.

Next turn the chair (a sofa or love seat is handled the same way)

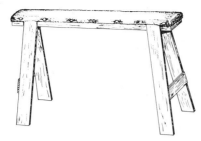

Fig. 2-1.   A padded upholstery trestle speeds work and simplifies handling.

Fig. 2-2.   Ripping chisels often have claws for pulling tacks.

Fig. 2-3.   A rawhide mallet helps prevent dents and scratches.

upside down on the bench or trestles and start the stripping process. Take a ripping chisel and grasp the butt end in your hand not just with your fingers. Fig. 2–2. Use a mallet in your other hand to tap the chisel. Fig. 2–3. Hold the mallet by the end of the handle in the same way you do the chisel. See Fig. 2–4. If you learn to hold the tools in this way you will have better control and more force when you use them.

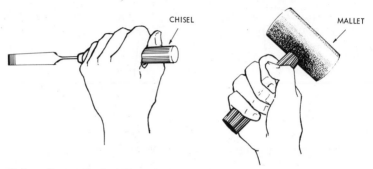

CHISEL

MALLET

Fig. 2-4. Correctly holding tools speeds work and prevents accidents.

You may find that the chair you are working on has staples holding the cambric and other fabrics to the frame. These staples are put in by power staple guns and may be much harder to pry out than tacks. To remove a staple place one corner of the ripping tool under the center of the staple and tap the handle with the mallet. Push down to pry out the staple.

If the ripping tool does not fit under the staples very well you may be able to make a staple puller by grinding or filing an old screwdriver so the point fits under the staple. This is driven under the staple with the mallet and the staple pried out. Be sure that the screwdriver is no longer being used for screws and that it has an unbreakable handle that can be hammered without damage. Never use a good screwdriver for pulling tacks, nails, or staples or it will be ruined for use on screws. Small chisels can be used like screwdrivers for getting under staples. The same precaution applies to them too. They are ruined for other work. Special tools for pulling staples can be obtained from manufacturers.

Sometimes one leg of a staple will stick or break off. Use a pair of pliers to remove these. Put the jaws of the pliers straight down on the staple. Grasp the handles as tight as possible so the staple is firmly gripped. Then push down on the handles until the side of the pliers rolls on the wood and the old staple is pulled out. If the broken part of the staple is too small to be grasped by the pliers take a hammer and drive the staple so it is completely buried in the wood. Small pieces of metal like this can cut and tear new material, and more importantly, can cause bad scratches on your hands when you are working on the frame.

REMOVE THE CAMBRIC

The cambric which is the last item to be put on is taken off first. This is the black cloth that covers the bottom of the chair or sofa. Fig. 2–5. The cambric is fastened all around the bottom of the frame. Pry out the tacks or staples that hold it in place. Tacks are removed in the same way as staples. The point of the ripping tool is placed against the head of the tack and the handle is tapped with the mallet. As the handle is tapped it is pushed down so the tack is popped out of the wood.

When the cambric has been removed throw it away. Also throw away

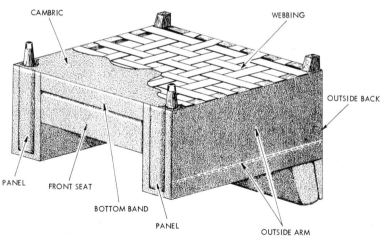

Fig. 2-5. Follow the steps in stripping a chair or sofa. Watch the construction as you work.

the tacks. You will do a much better job if you start with new materials. Be sure to place old tacks and other scrap in a tight waste container according to instructions in the school or shop. Next, remove the front panels if the chair has them. These are separate pieces of wood covered with fabric and fastened to the front of the arms to cover the seams. Slide the chisel between the panel and the arm front. Push the chisel toward the arm front to loosen the tacks. Pull off the panel using the chisel to loosen any stubborn tacks.

The outside back is taken off now. Start at the bottom. Fig. 2-5. Pay attention to the ways used to fasten the fabric. Tacks are used at the bottom. Cardboard tacking strips may be used at the top and sides. Note how the seams are sewed so the stitches do not show. Noticing these details will help later on when you are finishing the chair.

In removing the outside back cover you will need a sharp knife or a pair of sharp pointed scissors to cut the threads and twine used in sewing the seams. These threads are quite strong and a sharp edge will be needed to cut them. Seams that are sewed will usually be found along the outside back and arms. The knife or scissors will also be needed to cut the twines holding the springs in place when they are removed later. Seams that are sewed so that no stitches or threads show are called blind seams. The method of blind sewing these seams is described in detail in Chapter 8.

STRIPPING AN OUTSIDE ARM

The outside arm covering is removed from the bottom first. The outside arm may extend up to the top of the arm in some styles or it may stop part way, where the broken line is in Fig. 2-5. In other styles the inside arm curves over the top of the arm and under it back to the frame where the outside arm starts. The top of the outside arm is usually blind tacked. That is the fabric has been tacked with the outside facing the frame and then folded back over the tacked part to cover the tacks. Cardboard strips are used to make a straight edge and keep the tacks from cutting the cover.

The sides of the outside cover may be blind tacked or they may be blind sewed to the arm front and the outside back. You may need a sharp knife or a pair of pointed, sharp scissors to cut the twine holding the outside arm to the arm front. This is termed blind sewing and you will use it later on in finishing your chair. (See Chapter 8.) Notice how the thread does not show yet holds the fabric securely in place.

If the outside arm extends to the top of the arm you will see a lot of material on top of the frame where the wooden rail is padded. Study this to see how many layers of material there are and the kind of material used in them. In this padding you may find curled hair, cotton, rubberized hair, rubber or plastic foam, muslin, and other materials. The bottom band and the front seat are generally removed next. Then the inside arms, inside back and seat. Keep on until you have nothing left but the wooden frame.

Do not save any of the old fabric or materials. You may have heard that the old materials might be used for measuring or as patterns. However, these points will be covered with illustrations and diagrams that will simplify the procedures. It is much easier to measure new materials using a ruler than to try to get accurate measurements from old materials that have been stretched and worn.

If you are working on a channel back, tufted back, or some special design study the construction when you remove the old materials. This will help you to understand the instructions.

When the frame has been cleaned of all old materials inspect for large holes and fill with plastic wood. Sandpaper all rough surfaces where tacks or staples were pulled. Tighten screws in all joints where they are used. If the joints of the frame are loose use the mallet and try to open them up by tapping lightly. Apply new woodworking glue and clamp the joints until the glue sets. Sometimes adding a corner block will help prevent joints from working loose. Cut a block to fit the corner and then glue and screw it to the frame. Be sure to use hardwood such as maple and drill holes for the screws to avoid splitting the wood. Use large screws and drive them securely into the frame.

Rails that have a great many tack holes can be reinforced by adding a new tacking rail on the inside. See Chapter 3 for details.

Be sure to study the illustrations and the questions on page 14.

QUESTIONS FOR STUDY

1. Name the tools used in stripping furniture.
2. What order is used in stripping? Where do you start?
3. Which materials are saved? Why?
4. What should you watch for in stripping?
5. What is left on the frame after stripping?
6. What do you do if a staple breaks off in the rail?

Renewing the Frame

Chapter 3

RENEWING AND RESTYLING THE FRAME

When the frame has been stripped of the old upholstery the work of renewing the frame for the new upholstery begins. In renewing the frame there are two major operations to be covered. The first is to make the frame structurally sound and usable and the second is to give a new appearance to the exposed wood surfaces.

In renewing the frame the first step is to inspect all parts carefully. Study the drawings in Fig. 3–1 and 3–2 and learn the names of the parts of the frame. You will be seeing these names again and again so learn them thoroughly and you will know what is meant when they are used.

When you inspect the parts of the frame look for:

Split or crooked rails,

Loose screws,

Loose or wobbly corners,

Weak joints,

Rough spots or splinters,

Nails, and

Rails with a great many nail holes.

REPAIRING THE FRAME

Before doing any work on the frame be sure that all tacks, staples, and clips have been removed. Broken off legs of staples should be driven below the surface of the wood if they cannot be removed.

Holes along the rails should be filled with plastic wood. All screws

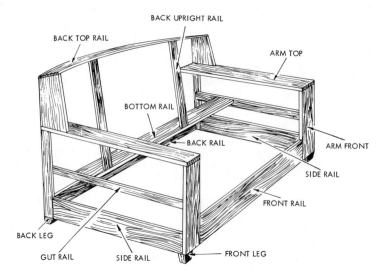

Fig. 3-1.　The parts of a chair frame.

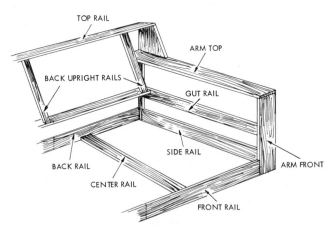

Fig. 3-2.　The parts of a sofa frame.

should be tightened and any very loose ones should be removed and replaced with slightly larger ones that will hold better. If there are any nails in the frame be sure to replace them with screws. Use a screw slightly larger than the nail and screw it in the nail hole.

Weak joints and loose corners are best taken apart and reglued. Instructions for this operation are given in detail in the description of converting a sofa into a love seat.

Cracked rails or those that have a great many nail and tack holes should have a new tacking rail added. This is done by putting a new rail inside of the old one and fastening the upholstery materials to it.

In obtaining wood for a new tacking rail, or for any use on a furniture frame, the worst mistake would be to use some lumber that might be on hand. Lumber used in furniture must withstand enormous amounts of strain and pressure. Softwoods, like pine and fir, will not do. You must use hardwood. Unless you can match the lumber in the frame be sure to use maple or ash.

Measure the old rail in thickness, depth, and length. Make the new rail the same size or a little smaller so that it will fit against the old rail tightly. Cover the new rail with a good quality wood glue and place it against the old rail with the tacking edge flush with the old rail. This will be either the bottom edge or the outside edge depending on where the rail is. Clamp with gluing clamps until the glue sets. Screw the two rails together with four wood screws that are about $1\frac{3}{4}$ inches long.

Be sure to drill small pilot holes so the screws will not split the wood. Use a little bar soap or oil on the threads to make them work easier in the hardwood. Sometimes rubbing a screw through the hair will add enough oil to make it turn easier if soap or oil is not handy.

Sand all rough surfaces with a sanding block or sandpaper. When you finish the frame will be sound and smooth.

Remember that wherever you added a new tacking rail you measure to it and not the old one. Generally this will mean adding about another inch to the measurements.

Check the frame for rigidity, smoothness, trueness to form. Corners should be tight and the frame should rest level.

RESTYLING THE FRAME

Frame restyling is an art in itself. However, there are many aspects of restyling and you can actually convert a chair into a chaise lounge or a sofa into a love seat without much difficulty. Often a simple cut here and there will convert the arm of a chair into a completely different shape and style. There is a mistaken idea that remodeling is a difficult task. The truth is that some remodeling or restyling can be very simple and inexpensive.

In remodeling or restyling a frame the upholsterer should be guided by the nature and extent of the work to be done. If the change can be made without extensive work the upholsterer should do it. However, extensive restyling or rebuilding of a major nature should be done by skilled frame makers.

Before making any changes in the frame study several catalogs and magazines to find styles that will be satisfactory and that can be used as models.

You may find that by merely removing the wings you can change a provincial style into a Lawson. Taking off the curved wood that forms the foundation for a rounded back, see Fig. 3–5, will give a straight line across the back that is currently in style.

Some examples are given of simple remodeling and restyling that can be done by the upholsterer to improve the comfort and style of the furniture.

REMODELING A CHAIR INTO A CHAISE LOUNGE

Comfortable chairs can be made even more so by converting them into chaise lounges when they are being reupholstered. Any style can be converted quite simply and easily.

To convert a chair into a chaise lounge first measure the width of the chair from the outside of one arm to the outside of the other arm. This is line A in Fig. 3–3 and is the width of the lounge. Next measure the length from the front rail to whatever length is wanted. This is line B in the figure.

Measure the side rails of the chair for depth and thickness. (This is generally $1\frac{1}{4}$ inches by $3\frac{1}{2}$ or $4\frac{1}{2}$ inches.) Obtain hardwood that

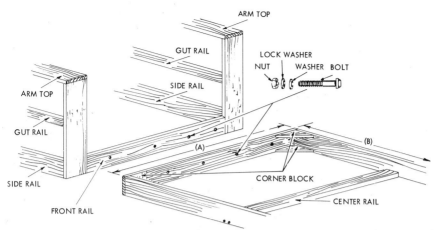

Fig. 3-3.   Steps in restyling a chair to a chaise lounge.

matches this in size. You will need three pieces that are the width of
the chair, line A in Fig. 3–3, and two that are the length of the extension
wanted, line B. Also obtain some extra wood of the same kind to make
corner blocks.

You will need two legs that match the ones on the front of the chair
in height and style. You can put four legs on the extension and not
fasten it permanently to the chair frame. This will make a matching
ottoman out of it.

The legs on the chair are moved forward so that they are centered
under the extension and the chair frame so that both parts are supported. Fig. 3–4. This reduces strain on the bolts holding the two
frames together.

The extension can be held together with dowels or wood screws. If
you use screws be sure to get ones that are are large enough to hold
the wood and to take the strain. Number 10 or 12 about 2 inches long
should be right.

There are four bolts that hold the frame for the extension and the

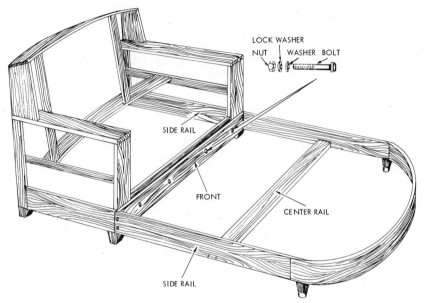

LOCK WASHER
NUT | WASHER BOLT

SIDE RAIL

FRONT

CENTER RAIL

SIDE RAIL

Fig. 3-4.   Finished extension for a chaise lounge.

chair frame together. This should be enough. Use bolts that are $\frac{1}{2}$ by three inches. If you use machine bolts place a flat washer under the head end and a lock washer under the nut end. You can use carriage bolts which do not require a washer at the head end. The washers prevent the bolts from sinking into the wood. When the extension has been fastened to the chair refinish the legs on both the chair and extension.

The upholstering is carried out in the same way as for the seat. This is described later on.

The curved end shown in Fig. 3–4 should be obtained from a lumber and millwork company or a furniture manufacturer.

Assembling the extension consists largely of having the right dimensions and of making the corners square. Use glue where the wood meets and then use two large screws at each corner or joint. Drill a pilot hole first. Clamp the frame so it is perfectly square and then add corner blocks as shown in Fig. 3–3. The corner blocks must be absolutely square so they will fit tightly into the corner and prevent wobbling. Place glue on the blocks and then screw them in place with two wood screws, one in each side. Blocks like this can be used to reinforce any corner of the chair. The blocks extend about three inches along each side and have a hole drilled through each side to hold a screw. Glue is used on the block to hold it more firmly to the frame and prevent movement.

The third piece of wood cut to the width of the chair is used as a center brace. It is fastened to the two side rails about half way between the ends of the extension. Fig. 3–4.

CONVERTING A SOFA INTO A LOVE SEAT

In many instances sofas that are not in the latest style or ones that take too much room can be remodeled into smaller sizes or into love seats with a little work. The frame of the sofa shown in Fig. 3–5 is that of a wing type, however, the same procedure is used on any sofa regardless of the style or size.

The first decision is on the width of the desired love seat. Any size can be used if a particular location needs a special size. Generally, four and one-half feet is considered to be the most desirable width for the average love seat.

Measure off this distance, or any other that you might want to use, on the front rail, top rail, bottom rail, and back rail as shown in Fig. 3–5. Be sure to use a try square for marking across the fronts of the rails and be sure that the marks are all in a straight line from the top rail to the front rail.

Start with the front rail and saw along the mark. Be careful to hold the saw straight and keep right on the pencil mark. Next cut the bottom rail and then cut the back rail. Finally, saw the top rail and the sofa is in two parts.

Now remove the rails on the short section of the sofa. These are marked (remove) on the illustration. When you remove the top and bottom rails you will find an upright rail between them. Remove this rail and save it for use later on. Discard the other rails.

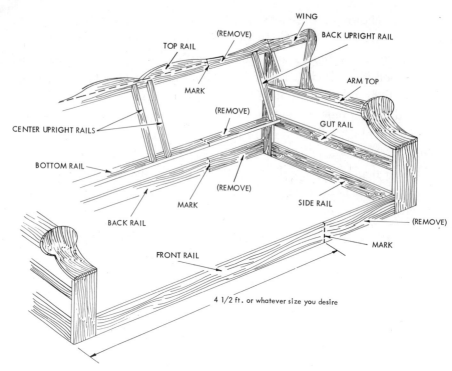

WING

(REMOVE)

TOP RAIL

BACK UPRIGHT RAIL

MARK

ARM TOP

(REMOVE)

CENTER UPRIGHT RAILS

GUT RAIL

BOTTOM RAIL

(REMOVE)

MARK

SIDE RAIL

BACK RAIL

(REMOVE)

FRONT RAIL

MARK

4 1/2 ft. or whatever size you desire

Fig. 3-5.   Restyling a sofa into a love seat.

In removing the rails you should work carefully to pull them straight out from the arm assembly. Tap on them to loosen the glue holding the dowels in place. Be careful to avoid twisting or forcing the rails or you may split the wood of the end. Also you may be able to save the dowels that are used to hold the frame together. If you are careful and fortunate most of the dowels may remain in the arm portion. Any dowels that break off in the arm should be drilled out. Measure the dowels and use a drill bit of the same size and an electric drill. Hold the drill so it is perfectly straight and drill out the broken dowel. In case you have not done this before the easy way is to saw off the broken part of the dowel as close to the rail as possible. Then use an awl or a punch to make a small hole in the very center of the sawed end. Use this hole as a starting place for the drill. Drill the hole to the depth of the dowels being used. Dowel drilling guides can be used and will save time and increase accuracy in making the holes.

Put a new dowel of the same size and length of the old one in the hole so that it sticks out the same distance as the others. Cover the new dowel and the inside of the hole with a good wood glue and tap the dowel into the frame.

Now put the arm assembly against the rest of the sofa. Line the long rails up with the arm assembly and carefully mark the places where the dowels will go into them. When you marked these places make a small hole in the exact place where the dowel will go and drill it just a little longer than the length of the dowels sticking out from the arm assembly. Be sure the holes are absolutely straight.

Take the upright rail that you removed when you cut off the top and bottom rails. Mark on the rails where this will go on the remodeled sofa. Place it in the same position as it was before. Drill new holes in the top and bottom rails. Now remove the two center upright rails by spreading the top and bottom rails apart some or saw the dowels with a fine blade saw. Drill out the ends in the upright rails and put in new ones. Move these two upright rails to the center of the shortened rails and make dowel holes in the rails so that they can be inserted there.

When all of the dowel holes have been drilled in the long rails and the dowels are in place on the upright rails and in the arm assembly you are ready to assemble the frame. Before doing this obtain some long gluing clamps that will go completely across the frame from end to end. Generally clamps six feet long will be right. You should use three of these for best results. Before putting the frame back together be sure to check the joints on the other end. They may have been loosened by use or from the work being done on the other end. Open up any joints that are loose and reglue them.

Now coat the dowels on the upright rails and the dowel holes that they fit into on the top and bottom rails with glue and put them together. Use a rawhide or rubber mallet to tap on one rail and then the other so the dowels go into the holes evenly and do not strain the wood. When these upright rails have been set in place coat the dowels on the arm assembly and the holes in the long rails with glue and then assemble the frame. Tap opposite each of the rails in turn. First one then the next and so on so that each part of the frame moves in gradually without twisting or springing the frame. Tap on the outside of the arm assembly opposite the dowels. When the dowels have been driven into the rails completely fasten the frame with the gluing clamps and let set for at least five hours.

If the back has curved top pieces as shown in Fig. 3–5, they should be removed and replaced in the center of the shortened frame. When you are remodeling the frame for length you can also remove these curved top pieces or the wings and restyle the frame into a different design.

This same procedure can be used on any style or size sofa to convert it to a love seat or a smaller size.

REMODELING A SOFA INTO A SECTIONAL COUCH

Sofas of any length or shape can be easily made into two piece sectional couches.

The first step is find the exact center of the sofa frame. Measure from arm to arm and mark the center on the front, back, bottom and top rails. Use a square to make straight lines on the face of the rails. Fig. 3–6.

Obtain two new center rails. These should be hardwood of the same kind as the frame if you can match it. Otherwise use maple or ash. These rails should be the same width and thickness as the side rails and just long enough to fit snugly between the front rail and the back rail. Place one on each side of the center mark so that there is about a one-quarter inch of space between them. Fasten these center rails to the front and back rails with glue and two strong wood screws at each rail as shown in Fig. 3–7.

Mark the bottom rail $1\frac{1}{4}$ inches on each side of the center mark. See Fig. 3–6. This will give a space of $2\frac{1}{2}$ inches between the marks. Saw the bottom rail on these marks. This will also let you remove the single upright back rail. Obtain two new upright center back rails.

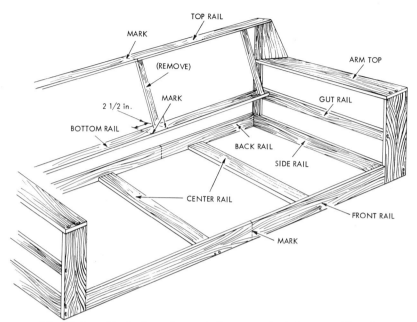

Fig. 3-6.   First steps in restyling a sofa into a sectional.

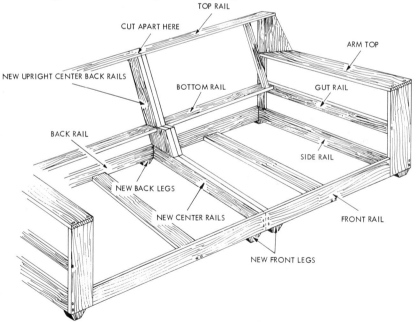

Fig. 3-7.   Final steps in restyling a sofa into a sectional.

These will go from the top rail, through the gap in the bottom rail to the back rail and the two new center rails. Fig. 3–7. These rails should be the same size wood as the new center rails and the same kind. Be sure to measure carefully and cut the rails to fit tightly against the top rail and the new center rails. Fasten them in place with glue and wood screws as you did the center rails across the seat. Be sure to allow about a quarter inch space between the rails.

Reinforce the joints at the two new rails by using a piece of plywood that is $\frac{1}{2}$ inch thick and four inches by eight inches. Glue this to the joint and hold with four $1\frac{1}{2}$ inch wood screws at each joint.

Next put on four new legs, two front and two back ones. Be sure the new legs match the ones on the sofa in height and style. Fig. 3–7.

Use a handsaw to cut the front rail between the new center rails. Next cut the top rail between the two new rails and then cut the back rail. The sofa is in two sections. Finish the frame by using glue and two wood screws to fasten each new upright center rail to the bottom rail.

REFINISHING EXPOSED WOOD SURFACES

Wood refinishing is an art in itself and a great deal of skill and experience is needed to do a first class job on fine wood finishes. However, most upholstered furniture has no large areas or complicated finishes so the basic procedures of refinishing these places are easily learned.

A question that sometimes arises from students is why go to the trouble of refinishing the few pieces of wood on the furniture, some of which do not show anyhow. The answer is that you are doing a complete job of reupholstering and every detail may be important at some time. There is also the possibility that you may come across some of the styles of furniture that do use wood as accents along the arms and seats and you will have to know how to finish these surfaces correctly.

The items that you need in refinishing a single chair in class should be obtained in the smallest quantities available. The items you will need are: rubber gloves, paint or varnish remover, set of bleaching solutions, an old brush, fine and medium grade sandpaper, rough steel wool, wood stain preferably with sealer, and either lacquer or boiled linseed oil.

Choose a leg and use the brush to cover it with the paint remover. Do just one leg at a time to avoid having the remover dry. When the remover has been on the wood two to three minutes wipe or scrape it off before it sets hard. Apply more coats until you have finally removed all of the old finish. In removing the last application of remover use steel wool soaked in water. This will clean off the old finish and also open the pores of the wood. Do this on all surfaces even though a putty knife or scraper was used to take the varnish remover off flat surfaces. Sanding will be much easier on the washed surfaces.

When the legs have been cleaned of the old finish put on the first solution of the bleaching kit. Soak the leg thoroughly with the bleaching solution. Let this dry for the recommended time given on the package and then apply the second solution. Let this dry over night. The next day the wood should be white and clean as if fresh from the mill. If one treatment does not remove all of the stain repeat the process.

Inspect the surface after the old finish has been removed and the wood bleached. If there are gashes in the wood take medium grade sandpaper and rub these areas until the gash disappears. After removing the deep gashes go over the entire surface with the fine sandpaper. Be sure to sand with the grain for a smooth finish. When the surface is smooth to the touch dust it to remove any sand or dust.

Now stain the wood. Work the stain into the wood thoroughly and then wipe off the excess with a piece of muslin. After the stain is dry finish the surface by spraying with a plastic finish or lacquer or cover with linseed oil and rub to a glossy finish.

Several outstanding stains have been introduced within the last few years. These contain sealers and are highly recommended for both amateurs and professionals. Always be sure that the stain is thoroughly dry before putting on finishing materials whether plastic, lacquer, or oil.

QUESTIONS FOR STUDY

1. What is the first step in converting a chair into a chaise lounge?
2. How much lumber is needed for a chaise lounge addition?

3. What is the usual width of a love seat?
4. What type of joints must be used?
5. Where are the new rails placed in making a sofa into a sectional?
6. List the lumber needed by quantity and use in making a sectional.
7. Why should legs and other exposed wood surfaces be refinished before starting the upholstering?
8. Give the underlying reason for refinishing the wood surfaces.
9. What precaution should be used to prevent screws from splitting the frame?
10. What should you keep in mind when obtaining wood for furniture?
11. Why are washers used on bolts holding the chaise lounge?

Building
the
Foundation

Chapter 4

SPRING TYPES AND USES

For many years all upholstered furniture depended on coil springs in the foundation to give softness to the seat and back.

The great expansion of the automobile and transportation fields created a demand for hundreds of thousands of upholstered seats a year. This huge demand could not be filled by skilled upholsterers using hand methods and the industry was forced to develop other methods that could be adapted to factory production using machine operators instead of skilled hand craftsmen.

In exploring ways to produce upholstered seats quickly and inexpensively many methods and materials were developed and a number of them have become useful in the custom furniture field. Some methods are suitable only for factory use where machines are available (Fig. 4–1) while others have become standard in all size shops.

Today there are several spring types that are used in upholstering work. The choice of the type is influenced by the space available for the springs, the size of the frame, and the method of fastening. Some springs may require about 10 inches of depth and others may need only 4 inches. Economy and speed of installation are other factors that have a bearing on the choice of springs. Some furniture is designed so that only one type of spring can be used. In many cases a choice can be made and the upholsterer must decide which one to use.

Some experts feel that the old type of double coil spring mounted on webbing and tied with twine gives the most comfortable foundation as there is a greater amount of springiness in all of the materials used

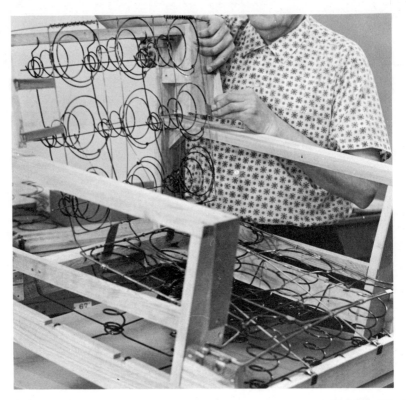

Fig. 4-1. Factories may use metal ties on springs.

as well as a greater depth. Others feel that the springs in the foundation are less important than the cushion in providing comfort and that any type of spring when well installed will give satisfactory service if combined with a good cushion.

In any case of upholstering be sure to look over the kind of spring in use to determine if that type must be used or if another would be suitable. Time, costs, and ease of installation should be considered in making a choice.

The main types of springs used in upholstered furniture are shown in Fig. 4-2.

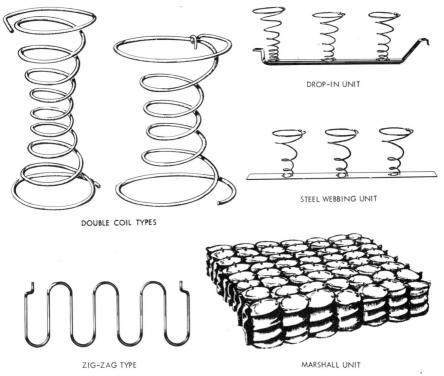

DROP-IN UNIT

STEEL WEBBING UNIT

DOUBLE COIL TYPES

ZIG-ZAG TYPE

MARSHALL UNIT

Fig. 4-2. Types of springs used in upholstered furniture.

Double coil springs have an hour-glass shape, that is the center coils are smaller than the top and bottom ones.

Single coil springs are cone-shape and fastened to a metal bar like springs in a bed. (Also called Drop-in units.)

Marshall units have each spring enclosed in a muslin sleeve. The sleeves are fastened together to make complete units for seats or backs.

Sinuous coil or zig-zag springs are made of heavy wire bent into a series of curves.

Some furniture uses other types of springs as in sofa bed styles where the springs for the bed form the foundation for the seat. These often use a metal mesh with small coil springs along the sides and ends. Metal frame furniture may use this type of spring or a zig-zag type.

In some cases special machine-made springs may be used and these would need to be replaced with one of the types listed above as the machine-made springs are made especially for one size of furniture and are not available except on special order.

SELECTING COIL SPRINGS

Whenever possible coil springs should be selected to suit the weight of the persons who are going to use the furniture. This can be done in custom upholstering or reupholstering when the family that uses the furniture is definitely known. In manufacturing for general sale, as in stores, an average weight has to be assumed and the springs selected for the average weight.

Springs come in soft, medium, and hard types. The difference is due to gage of wire, size of coils, height, and several other factors. In general, a coil spring with small center coils will be firmer or have a harder feel than one with larger center coils. A higher spring is usually firmer than a lower one of the same diameter. The thickness or gage of the wire is another factor. A thicker wire will be firmer than a thinner or lighter gage one. Manufacturing firms vary in the sizes they make and sell so the selection of springs should be made of the ones available from your source of supply.

Some manufacturers use a coil count as a basis of coil size. Five coils are counted from the bottom of the spring. The number remaining above that determines the number of the spring. Thus a number four size has four coils above the first five or nine altogether. A number five has five coils above the first five or ten coils. Other manufacturers base spring size on the weight and number of springs per pound. Find out the system used by your source of supply and follow that.

Seat and back springs have top and bottom sides. The bottom may have a slightly smaller diameter than the top. Also the top has the end of the wire either turned in or knotted around the coil. This is to prevent the end of the spring from pushing through the padding and cover. Cushion springs have both sides the same.

The single cone type that is generally available to the custom upholsterer is the drop-in type. This usually has three springs mounted on a steel bar. The bar has the ends shaped so that they will fit over the chair rails and are nailed or screwed in place. This type can be used on furniture with narrow rails as the bar drops down several inches below the top of the rails. The top of these units must be hand tied. The saving is in eliminating the webbing and in providing a longer lasting support to the springs.

Marshall units are manufactured by enclosing small size springs in muslin cases or bags. These bags are made in rows and the rows are fastened together with metal links called hog rings. Generally enough rows are fastened together to form a back, seat, or cushion. Where more height or width is needed than the standard sizes provide the rows are separated by cutting the hog rings and then adding one or more rows and fastening to the standard unit by hog rings or by sewing. The Marshall units are used with webbing.

The sinuous coil, zig-zag, or No-Sag springs are useful in places where depth is important. The spring is a strong wire formed into a series of rounded curves. When this is fastened to a frame the wire stretches so a spring action occurs. The degree of springiness is controlled by the gage of the wire and the amount of curve used in mounting the spring. Letting the center of the spring curve up gives more softness while stretching it tight reduces it. Small coil springs are used to stabilize the zig-zag springs and to keep padding from falling through. Special clips are used to secure the ends of the springs. Only a minimum of two inches depth is needed to install these springs.

APPLYING THE WEBBING

The most important procedure in upholstering is that of applying the webbing correctly. The webbing serves as the support for the seat and back and the entire success of the upholstering depends on the webbing being placed right and performing its function.

To apply webbing you will need furniture or spring webbing of 10 oz weight, 16 oz size tacks, 6 oz size tacks, a webbing stretcher, and a magnetic head tack hammer. Fig. 4-3.

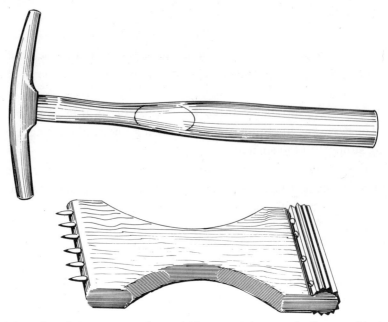

Fig. 4-3.   A tack hammer and a webbing stretcher are indispensable tools.

Turn the chair or couch so it is upside down and supported on the trestles at a convenient height. Find the center of the frame and mark it on the front and back rails. Take the end of the webbing and place it on the center mark on the bottom of the front rail. Make sure the webbing extends evenly on each side of the center. Then fold over an inch of the webbing and tap it lightly with the hammer so it stays folded. Drive four of the 16 oz tacks into the rail toward the inside edge. Space the tacks as evenly as possible across the webbing. Next drive three more tacks toward the outside of the rail so they are spaced between the other four. This gives a staggered effect and helps prevent splitting or weakening of the rail. If the rail shows signs of splitting try using 12 oz tacks. In extreme cases you may have to add a tacking rail as explained in the discussion of repairing the frame in Chapter 3.

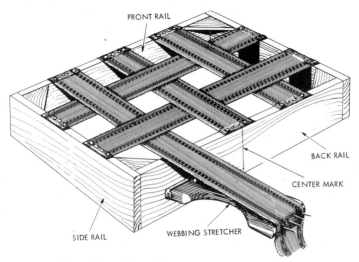

BACK RAIL

CENTER MARK

SIDE RAIL   WEBBING STRETCHER

Fig. 4-4.   Stretching and tacking webbing.

The webbing is carried over the bottom of the back rail and centered over the center mark. The teeth of the webbing stretcher are hooked into the webbing so that the stretcher is on a 30° angle when the padded base is against the frame. Push down on the stretcher until the webbing is as tight as you can make it. This is described as being as tight as the head of a drum. Fig. 4–4.

Drive three tacks through the webbing while you have it stretched. Space these evenly across the webbing. Now cut off the webbing about an inch beyond the frame and fold this back over the tacks. Drive four more tacks through the two layers of webbing. The purpose of folding the webbing and tacking through it is to prevent the heads of the tacks from cutting the threads. Fig. 4–5.

The next strip of webbing is applied about an inch from the first one. Many upholsterers use their thumbs for measuring the spacing of the webbing. However, to be sure measure your thumb when it is

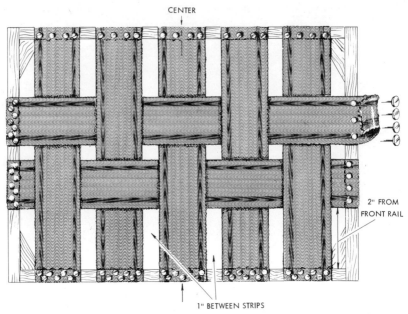

Fig. 4-5. Webbing pattern used for seats.

pressed down and see if it is about an inch wide. This spacing will give
five rows of webbing across a chair bottom.

When the five rows of webbing have been stretched and tacked securely from the front to the back rails go to the front of the chair and
run a strip of webbing from side rail to side rail. The strip is woven
through the tacked webbing about two inches from the front rail. Stretch
and tack the webbing the same as you did the strips going the other way.
Continue to weave other strips of webbing across the bottom until you
have covered the bottom of the seat. Fig. 4–5.

In many operations both hands are needed for stretching and smoothing materials. It is difficult to tack these securely if each tack has to be
placed on the hammer by hand. To speed up the tacking process many
upholsterers hold the tacks in their mouths and place them on the end

of the magnetic tack hammer with the tongue and lips. This is called "spitting tacks" in the trade. Upholsterer's tacks are sterilized for this reason.

The technique of spitting tacks is to place a small quantity of the right size in the mouth. These are moved over to one side in the cheek. Then, with the tongue, a tack is moved to the front of the mouth and manipulated so the head end is facing outward just beyond the lips. The magnetic head of the hammer is brought up to the tack and a spitting motion is used to put the tack on the head of the hammer.

A safer way than holding the tacks in the mouth, although somewhat slower, is to place the tacks in holes in a piece of cardboard where they can be picked up individually by the hammer. Be sure the holes are large enough to let the tacks move easily and small enough to hold them almost upright. The cardboard can be placed within convenient reach of the hand when tacking.

When the webbing for the seat has been completed the next step is to put webbing on the back and arms. Each arm gets two strips of webbing on the inside. Fig. 4–6. Six pieces of webbing are used on the back with three going across and three up and down. The webbing on the arms and back are tacked with 6 oz tacks. The webbing is stretched firmly but not as tight as on the seat. In all cases the webbing is folded back and most of the tacks placed through the folded part to prevent cutting the threads.

In webbing sofas and love seats the webbing going across the width of the bottom or back is tacked where it passes over the center rails that keep the frame from bending. Be sure to stagger these tacks.

Steel webbing is used where great durability is desired or where hard use and heavy loads may be expected. The steel may be used in place of the jute webbing. The ends of the springs are worked into the slots in the strip. Sometimes the steel strips are placed underneath the jute webbing to reinforce it and prevent sagging if the jute should break or wear out.

Steel webbing is also used to repair sagging springs when broken or loose webbing occurs. The steel webbing is placed under the jute and stretched until the springs are back in place. Then the webbing is nailed

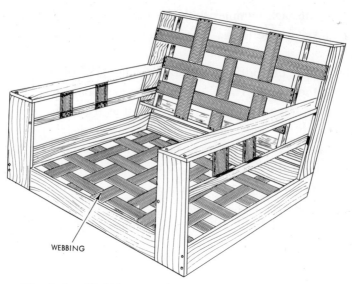

WEBBING

Fig. 4-6.   Webbing pattern used for arms and backs.

to the frame to keep the springs from sagging. A special stretcher is needed to grip the metal webbing and stretch it. Special nails are used to hold the steel webbing to the rails.

LOCK KNOT TIEING

Upholsterers, like sailors, have to be good at tieing knots. Knots are used constantly to attach the ends of twine and thread, to hold springs and fabrics in place, and to fasten many parts of the chair securely.

The lock knot is used to fasten the ends of twine to fabric or springs, to attach buttons, and to provide a means of tightening the twine. It is used constantly in upholstery and you should practice tieing this knot until you can tie it automatically. Other knots will be described where they are needed.

You will need to study the drawing as you read the instructions. There are four steps in tieing this knot and each one is shown in the illustration.

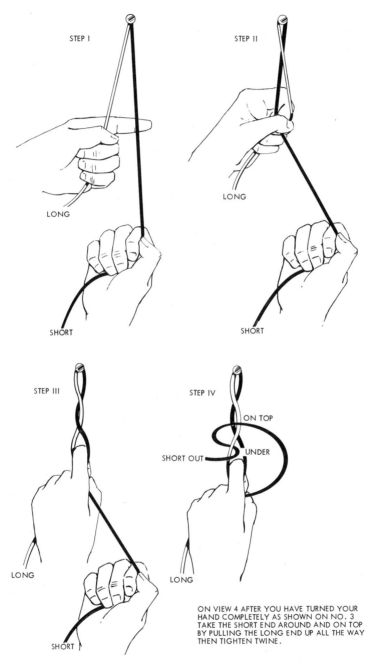

STEP I

STEP II

LONG

LONG

SHORT

SHORT

STEP III

STEP IV

ON TOP

SHORT OUT

UNDER

LONG

LONG

SHORT

ON VIEW 4 AFTER YOU HAVE TURNED YOUR
HAND COMPLETELY AS SHOWN ON NO. 3
TAKE THE SHORT END AROUND AND ON TOP
BY PULLING THE LONG END UP ALL THE WAY
THEN TIGHTEN TWINE.

Fig. 4-7. Steps in making a lock knot.

For practice take a piece of twine about 30 inches long and loop it around any convenient object or put a tack in a board and loop the twine around it. Have one end longer than the other but keep the short end about 10 inches long until you have mastered the process.

Take the long end in your left hand. This would be the twine attached to the needle when you are working. Take the short end with your right hand. Fig. 4–7, Step I.

Hook the short piece of twine with your left hand index finger and bring it under the long piece as shown in Fig. 4–7, Step II.

Now turn your left hand over with the twine still hooked in the index finger. Fig. 4–7, Step III.

Take the short end in your right and bring it over the two twines in your left hand. Then go under the twines and bring the short end up between the two twines as shown in Fig. 4–7, Step IV.

Take your index finger out of the twines and you have a knot that will slide along the long twine. This will enable you to tighten the twine. When the twine is tight and the knot is pulled as far as it will slide pull the short (or loose) end of the twine to lock the knot.

When you are using this knot with webbing, burlap, and cloth of any kind it is a good practice to place a small piece of cotton, about the size of a quarter dollar, in the loop just before you draw it tight. The cotton will prevent the knot from pulling out of the cloth by providing a larger holding area. This is especially true when you are attaching buttons. It is not necessary to use cotton in the knot if you are tieing the knot to a spring, edge wire, or something that it cannot pull out of.

This knot locks when it is tight and the short end is pulled hard. After locking the knot you can cut off any excess twine but be sure to leave a half inch or so close to the knot.

SEWING THE SPRINGS

When the webbing has been completely stretched on the seat you are ready to install the springs. The seat springs can be put on before you finish putting the webbing on the inside arms and back, but it is generally easier to do all the webbing at one time.

A chair seat requires nine springs spaced in three rows each way.

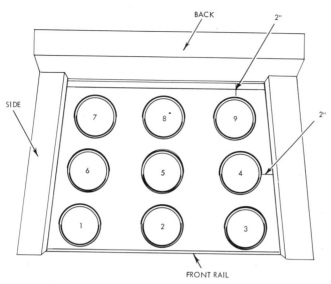

Fig. 4-8. Placing the springs on the seat.

The first row of springs is placed right up against the front rail with the right and left springs (numbered 1 and 3 in Fig. 4–8) about two inches from the side rails. The middle spring (2) is centered between the other two.

The other springs are placed so that there is two inches between each outside spring and the rail and even spacing with the other springs. The spacing is shown in Fig. 4–8.

When the springs have been placed mark around the bottom coil of each spring with chalk. This will help you in placing the springs in the right place when you sew them to the webbing as you will not have to remeasure to find the right place.

Thread a needle with a heavy thread such as upholstery #252. You can use either a straight needle or a curved one whichever you prefer. Some upholsterers use a double pointed needle for this work as you do not need to turn the needle while sewing. With the thread doubled start sewing the springs at a front outside corner. Push the needle up through

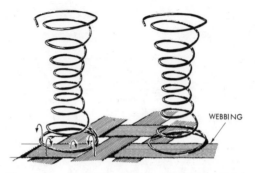

Fig. 4-9.　Sewing springs to the webbing.

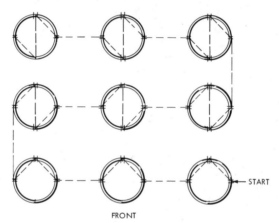

FRONT

Fig. 4-10.　Sewing pattern for the springs.

the bottom of the webbing right beside the bottom coil of the spring on the outside. Go to the inside of the coil and down through the webbing. See Fig. 4–9. Make a lock knot to hold the loop of twine tight against the spring and the webbing.

Now go across to the next spot shown on Fig. 4–10 and make another loop around the coil of the spring. When the needle is brought out through the webbing make a twist knot in the thread. This is done by twisting the thread three times around the needle before the thread is drawn tight. Then go to the next place on the spring shown on Fig. 4–10 and sew that to the webbing. Follow the diagram.

Three stitches are made on the front springs and four on the other ones. Each time a stitch is made it is knotted. Twist knots are used for all except the first and last stitches on the thread. Do not attempt to use enough thread for all the springs at one time or you will have so much that it will become tangled. Use enough thread for three or four springs. Start each new thread with a lock knot and end it with two twist knots.

In some shops and factories metal clips are used to hold the springs to the webbing. The clips are put on from the top and clinched in place by a special tool. This speeds the work of fastening springs considerably.

TIEING SEAT SPRINGS

Furniture springs must be fastened in place. This is quite simple where the bottoms of the springs are concerned. They are fastened to the webbing. The tops of the springs have several problems that must be solved. They have to be kept in place and at the same height. But they must be able to move up and down at the same time without getting out of line or pulling the other springs out of position.

These problems are overcome by tieing the springs so they cannot move sideways or too high but can move downward and remain in place.

In learning to tie springs you will have to learn several new knots and ways of fastening the heavy twine used. Study the drawings carefully and try to imagine what happens when the spring is pushed down. Then you will understand why the twine must be placed accurately.

Most springs will have an edge wire applied to them. If your particular style needs one be sure to stretch the front edges of the front springs to give more strength across the front. To do this take the top coil and pull it upward as hard as you can. After stretching the wire the spring should look like the front one in Fig. 4–21 and 4–22. It should be about an inch higher on the front side.

Before starting to tie the seat be sure that you have a tack hammer, 16 oz tacks, and a pound of seat springing twine. Some upholsterers use a lighter grade twine for the backs and the heavy grade for seat work.

Fig. 4-11. Measuring spring twine easily and quickly.

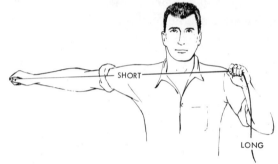

Fig. 4-12. Determining short and long ends for spring tieing.

Start the tieing from the back of the seat. First cut even lengths of twine for each row of springs. Generally you can measure the first length of twine by taking it in your fingers and stretching it between your widespread arms. Fig. 4–11. Double this and you will have a piece about 12 feet. Make three twines this long. Now find the point that is about $4\frac{1}{2}$ feet from one end and fold there. You can do this simply by holding the twine with a widespread arm and folding it at the opposite shoulder. Fig. 4–12.

Place two 16 oz tacks about a half inch apart on top of the back rail and opposite the center of each spring. Drive the tacks about half way in.

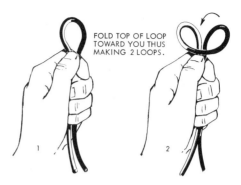

Fig. 4-13.　Making a tack loop.

FOLD TOP OF LOOP
TOWARD YOU THUS
MAKING 2 LOOPS.

Now take the loop where you folded the twine into two lengths and bring the loop toward you so that two loops are formed as in Fig. 4–13. Put these two loops over the tacks that you placed opposite the springs. Finish driving the tacks so the twines are held securely. Repeat this until each row of springs has a double twine in back of it.

There are several patterns used in tieing springs. The pattern recommended here is the sixteen way tie. It has the advantages of holding the springs at several levels and also securing them from any side movement. Another pattern is shown for tieing the back springs. This pattern is used by some upholsterers for the seat too.

Start with the shorter piece of twine. Bring this up to the third coil from the top of the spring and make a loop knot around the coil as shown in Figs. 4–14 and 4–15. In making this knot remember to pull the spring down to its finished height. This is about five inches above the top of the rail and will compress the spring slightly. The first twine is used to set the height of the springs and also to line them up.

Now make a loop knot around the top coil of the back spring on the inside. Go to the top coil of the center spring and make another knot at the back. Take the twine across to the front of the spring and tie it on the second coil from the top. The third spring is tied at the fourth coil at the back and at the front. The twine is brought out and anchored to the front rail by two turns around a tack which is then driven into

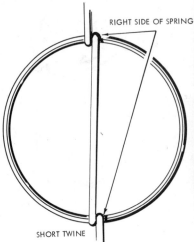

RIGHT SIDE OF SPRING

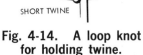

SHORT TWINE

Fig. 4-14. A loop knot for holding twine.

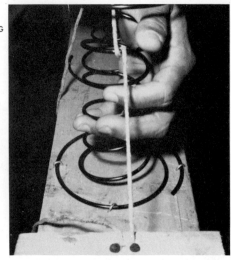

Fig. 4-15. A loop knot in place on a spring.

the rail. Fig. 4–22. Before anchoring the tack in the front rail check to see if the springs are all the same height except for the pulled up edge on the front one. If not loosen the knots and adjust them until all the springs are in a straight line and the same height.

The second piece of twine, the long end, is taken and fastened around the first by making a Y knot as shown in Fig. 4–16 and 17 at the back of the back spring on the third coil from the top. Fig. 4–23. This twine then goes up to the top coil at the back. This twine brings the back edge of the spring to the right height and there is an easy way to do this.

The twine is brought up on the outside of the top coil of the spring and a loop is made around the wire on the *left* side of the twine. This loop is pulled down until the spring is about five inches above the back rail. Pinch the loop tight with your fingers to hold the spring at this height. Then take the twine and go across and under the spring and

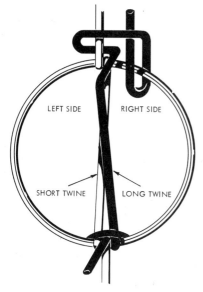

Fig. 4-16. A Y knot using two twines.

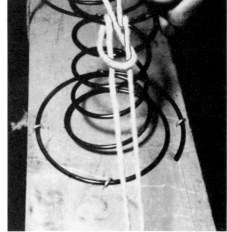

Fig. 4-17. A completed Y knot on a spring.

make another loop with the loop on the *right* side of the twine. Slide this loop around the spring until it meets the one that is being held. Bring the second loop up against the first one and tighten it as tight as you can. This will lock it and hold the spring at the right height. This knot is called a reverse Y knot or a clove hitch. See Figs. 4–18, 19, and 4–20.

The twine goes from the back of the spring to the top coil on the other side where it is tied around the other twine with a Y knot. It follows the first twine to the center spring and is tied front and back on the top coil also with Y knots as shown in Fig. 4–16 and 4–17. It follows the first twine to the fourth coil at the back of the front spring which is point B on Fig. 4–23. Then across the spring to the front of the fourth coil and over to the frame where it is tacked at point C. The twines are tied with a Y knot at each side of the spring.

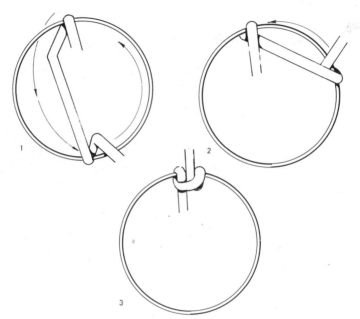

Fig. 4-18. A reverse Y or clove knot.

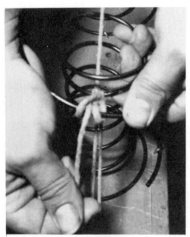

Fig. 4-19. Making a reverse Y knot.

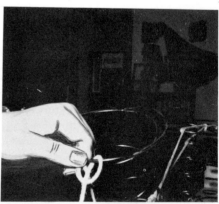

Fig. 4-20. The completed reverse Y knot.

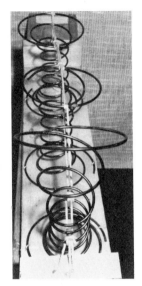

Fig. 4-21.   Seat spring showing raised front for added density.

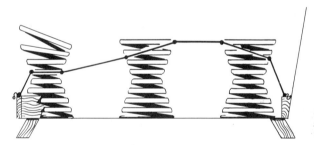

Fig. 4-22.   Holding the springs with the long twine.

The front edges of the springs along the front of the chair have been pulled up so they are about an inch higher than the rest of the springs. Stretching the front springs this way will more than triple the strength of the springs. This is the place that gets a great amount of weight and adding more tension to the spring by stretching it will help prevent the front edge from sagging. Figs. 4–21 and 4–22.

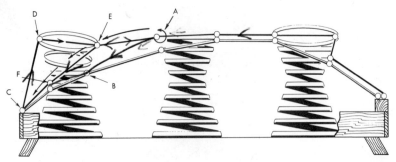

Fig. 4-23.   Setting and tieing seat springs with the second twine.

The long twine is brought up to the pulled up coil of the front spring from the tack, point D on Fig. 4–23. The twine is carried over the top of the spring wire and out on the left side of the twine. The twine is pulled down so the top of the spring is brought level with the rest of the springs in the seat. Pinch the twine where it crosses to keep it from slipping. With the other hand take the twine and bring it up under the spring to the right of the loop that is being held. Come around the spring to the left of the twine and pull the new loop up close to the one being held. This will lock the twine and hold the spring in place. This is the same reverse Y knot you made on the back coil.

The twine is carried across the spring to the back where a simple loop is made around the wire. Then the twine goes to the middle spring (A) where it is tightened to bring the front spring in line with the edge of the front rail. When the front spring has been lined up pinch the twine to prevent slipping and then complete a Y knot as shown in Fig. 4–16.

From the middle spring the twine goes back to the top of the front spring (E) where it is tied around the loop knot there with a Y knot that locks both twines. (Fig. 4–16). Then the twine drops down to the fourth coil (F) where a similar Y knot is made and then the twine goes to the tack rail and is tacked. This is repeated on all the rows of springs. Fig. 4–23.

Fig. 4-24.   Seat spring showing the completed ties.

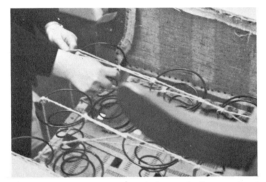

Fig. 4-25.   Completing the tieing of the seat springs.

The springs are now set in height and in straight rows from front to back. Fig. 4–24 and 25.

Next the springs are cross-tied from side to side. This operation uses a single twine. Measure by laying a length of twine across the frame on top of the springs from rail to rail and add about three-fourths more for tacking and tieing. This procedure is followed regardless of the size of the project. Use $1\frac{3}{4}$ times the length of the springing twine when it is laid on top of the distance it is to run.

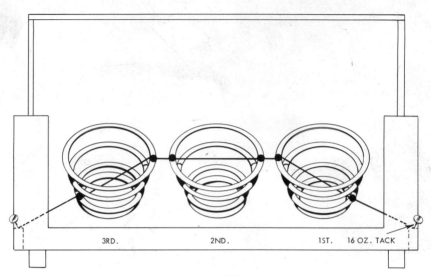

Fig. 4-26.   Cross tieing the springs.

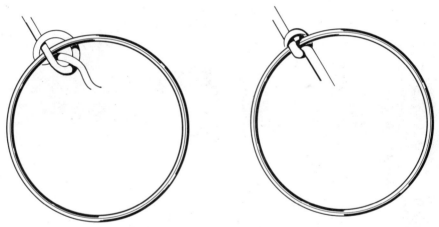

Fig. 4-27.   Steps in tieing a single twine lock knot.

Place a 16 oz tack in the side rail opposite the center of a row of springs. Wrap the twine around the tack twice and drive it down. Now go to the third coil of the spring and make a lock knot. Figs. 4–26 and 4–27.

Then go to the top coil on the opposite side and make another knot. Continue to tie the twine to the top coil of the center spring on both sides and to the inside of the top coil of the last spring. Then drop down to the third coil and tie it on the outside and tack the twine to the frame. Check to see that the springs are all the same height across the front. Repeat this same cross tie on the other two rows of springs.

The lock knot shown in Fig. 4–27 is used to tie twine whenever a single twine is used. Study the diagram carefully. The reverse Y or clove hitch is also recommended for single twines.

The springs are now tied from front to back and from side to side. They have been pulled down so the springs are the same height and in straight rows.

Next the diagonal ties are put in. Measure these as you did the cross ties. When starting a diagonal tie always go to the third coil of the spring next to the frame. Then go to the top and continue tieing to the top coils until you reach the last spring when you drop down again to the third coil again before tacking to the rail. Put diagonal ties in both directions. This will complete an eight-way tie as the springs are tied in eight different directions.

To make a sixteen-way tie four additional rows of twine are put in. Two run from back to front between the rows of springs and the other two run from side to side between the rows of springs. These additional rows do not tie to the springs but to the twines making up the eight-way tie. Fig. 4–28. These serve to distribute the weight and to serve as additional safeguards in case a twine breaks. Wherever twines cross they should be tied with a lock knot. The tension (pull) on each twine should be as nearly even as you can make it. If one is too loose or too tight, re-do it. Otherwise the tight twine will take all the strain and may break. A loose one is useless.

This completes the sixteen-way tie and only an edge wire is needed to complete the springs for the seat. Fig. 4–29.

The Y knot for locking two twines was illustrated in Fig. 4–16. This secures the twines so that both are held in case of one or the other breaking.

There are times when a lock knot is needed but there is no second

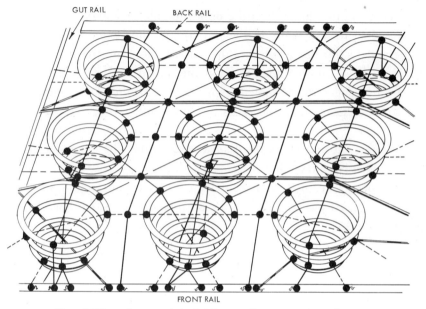

Fig. 4-28. A completed 16-way tie on seat springs.

Fig. 4-29. Tied springs showing twine and edge wire in place.

twine. This can be overcome by making a reverse Y knot which uses only one twine. The reverse Y is also called a clove hitch.

The fast and easy way to make this knot is to bring the twine over the top of the spring wire. Loop it under the wire to left. Pull this loop until the desired height of the spring is obtained or until the twine is as tight as you want it. Pinch the looped part of the twine together so it doesn't slip. Now go to the opposite side of the spring and make another loop but make this one from below the coil and on the right side of the twine.

Now take the last loop and slide it around the wire until it meets the other loop. Pull the loop tight and you have a reverse Y knot or a clove hitch. When this is pulled tight it holds the twine in both directions. It is an easy knot to undo and retie and it makes adjusting spring height and twine tension very simple. See Fig. 4–18.

APPLYING THE EDGE WIRE

Most chairs and sofas require an edge wire around the springs. A few styles do not. Sometimes an edge wire will be used only on the front and part of the sides, but this is a questionable practice and the edge wire should go completely around the springs for best results. Some backs also need an edge wire. Do not save the old edge wire, use a new one and bend it to fit the new springs. For applying the edge wire you will need a length of spring-type edge wire. This should be long enough to go completely around the outside edge of the springs with several inches extra for fastening the ends of the wire together. To find out the length of edge wire needed measure across the top of a row of springs from front to back. Be sure to measure to the outside of the top coils. Measure the same way across the springs from side to side. Double both figures and add about eight inches for joining the ends. This should be about 8 to 9 feet. Edge wire comes in several sizes and should be obtained in a size to fit your chair or sofa. The supplier of the wire should be able to give you the right size. In addition to the wire you will need some edge wire clips or Baker clips. While the edge wire can be tied to the springs the clips are easier to apply and make a good fastening. Clip pliers are available and whether you need a pair depends

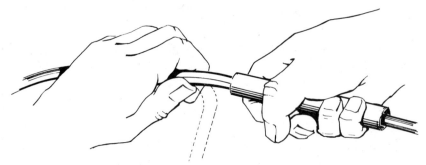

Fig. 4-30.   Bending an edge wire.

on the amount of upholstering you intend to do. Ordinary pliers can be used but they take more work and time than the special clip ones.

Also obtain a piece of $\frac{1}{4}$ inch pipe about five inches long.

To bend the wire place the thumb of your left hand on the wire at the point where the bend will be and grasp the wire firmly. Place the section of pipe over the wire by sliding it on from an end. Move the pipe up to within an inch of the point where your thumb is placed on the edge wire and then pull down sharply on the pipe. (See Fig. 4–30.) This will bend the wire at your thumb. Measure the distance where the next corner will be and place your thumb there. Bend the wire as before. Be sure to make the bends in the same direction so that a square is formed.

Place a clip over the edge wire and the front of each spring wherever they touch as shown in Fig. 4–31 and 4–32. Use several clips on the overlapped part of the edge wire at the back. Any extra wire should be cut off with a hacksaw or file.

Applying the edge wire before the springs are tied is sometimes recommended. While this can be done there are several objections to it. One is that the front springs are harder to set when they are all held together by the wire. Another is that the edge wire is in the way when tieing the springs. In applying the edge wire after the springs are tied

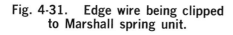
Fig. 4-31. Edge wire being clipped
to Marshall spring unit.

JOIN

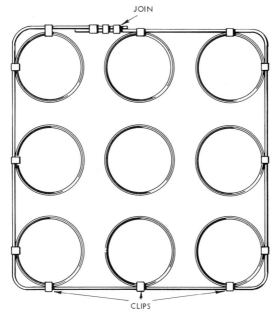

CLIPS

Fig. 4-32. Placing edge wire clips.

the wire serves to hold them in place and adds additional strength to
the whole seat.

The clips can be put on at one side or the other of the knots and
do not interfere with them. Certainly it is easier to apply clips with
the twine knotted to the springs than to knot the twine when the edge
wire is in place. Inasmuch as each spring has to be set in place individually by the twine it is less work to do so when each spring can
be handled separately.

Building the Foundation 57

TIEING SPRINGS ON INSIDE BACK

The inside back of a sofa or chair is covered with webbing in the same way as the seat. The webbing, however, does not need to be placed quite as close or stretched quite as tight as on the seat as there is less weight and strain on it. Generally three strips of webbing in each direction are enough for an average chair back.

Place the chair on its back and set the springs in place as shown in Fig. 4–23, 33 and 34. Use a crayon or chalk to mark the places on the webbing when the springs have been placed evenly. If an edge wire is going to be used as on a Lawson back the springs are spaced to within 2 inches of the frame on the outside. With a wing back, or pillow back, or some other style that does not need an edge wire the springs are placed about 5 inches from the frame.

Back springs are lighter in construction than seat springs. The number needed in a back depends on the height of the back. There are normally three rows across the back of a chair and about three high. A tall back type such as a wing may need two more rows in the height.

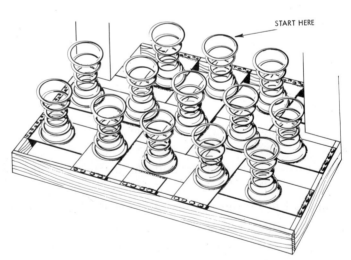

START HERE

Fig. 4-33. Placing back springs in position.

Fig. 4-34.   Sewing back springs to webbing.

Sew the springs to the webbing as you did in the seat with a needle, a medium size curved one may be best, and number 252 thread. Follow the same pattern in sewing the springs as in the seat using lock knots where needed and loop knots elsewhere.

Back springs are tied a little differently than seat springs as there is less weight to support. However, if you are remodeling or reupholstering for a heavy person's use you can use the same tie as in the seat. Generally an eight-way or diamond tie is satisfactory, Fig. 4–35, and only a single twine is used. You can use a lighter twine for back springs.

There are two ways of tieing the springs depending on the style of the back. In many cases the tie will be done as shown in Fig. 4–36. The tie next to the frame is made on the second coil and then the top coils across the back and down to the second coil on the opposite side. The top coils of the outside springs are bent up to give added tension. The twines are tied so that the finished height is about 4 inches above the frame. The twines run from bottom to top and from side to side diagon-

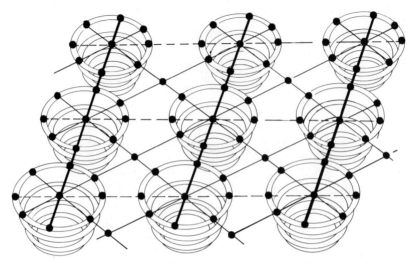

Fig. 4-35.   Diamond style tie for springs.

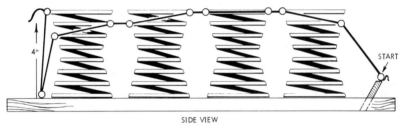

SIDE VIEW

Fig. 4-36.   Pattern of tieing springs for square edge style backs.

ally in both directions. The edge wire is applied to the springs, after tieing in the same way as the seat.

The other style, where an edge wire is not used, is shown in Fig. 4–37. In this style the springs are set in about 5 inches from the frame and the twine goes to the top of the coil nearest the frame. Also the outside coil

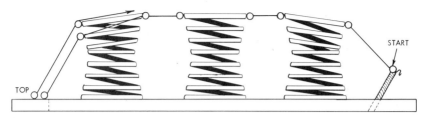

Fig. 4-37. Pattern of tieing springs for round edge style backs.

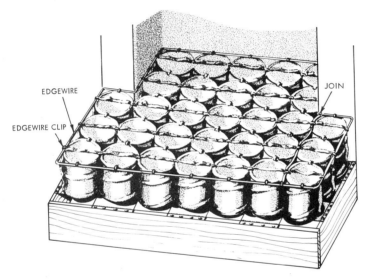

Fig. 4-38. Marshall spring unit in chair back.

Fig. 4-39. No-sag springs, clips, and stabilizer spring.

is not bent up to give added density. Otherwise the tieing is done in the same way as in the previous style.

Marshall units are used quite frequently for back springs. In some styles additional rows of springs will be needed and these are cut off in rows or sections to fill out the space. The extra rows are fastened to the unit with metal clasps or hog rings or by sewing them to the others. In sewing make several turns of the twine around each place where the springs touch. Be sure to knot the twine before and after making the connection of the two springs. An edge wire is clipped to the outer rows of the springs. Figs. 4–31 and 4–38.

If no-snag springs are used in the back they should be connected to the side rails with clips and to each other with stabilizing springs as shown in Fig. 4–39.

TACKING THE BURLAP

Burlap is used to cover the tied springs and the other openings in the frame and to serve as support for padding and the cover. The burlap should be good quality of 10 oz weight and must be securely fastened to the wood frame with 4 oz tacks.

Your first operation is to cut a piece of burlap about 2 inches wider on all sides than the opening to be covered. In measuring the opening be sure to include enough burlap for tacking to the frame. The additional 2 inches are added to this so a fold can be made all around the edge of the burlap to tack through. This prevents the heads of the tacks from cutting the threads and causing the burlap to tear.

Start with the seat, then do the inside back, next cover the inside arms, and finally cover the wings if the furniture has them.

Fold the burlap over about $\frac{3}{4}$ of an inch along the front of the seat. Tack through this to the top of the front rail. Be sure the burlap is centered and work from the center to the edges to prevent wrinkling. Space the tacks about $1\frac{1}{2}$ inches apart. Pull the burlap back over the springs to the back rail making sure that the burlap is smooth and tight but not so tight that it compresses the springs in any way. Tack the burlap to hold it in place then fold over the edge and finish tacking through the fold. Fig. 4–40.

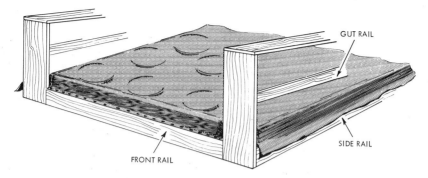

Fig. 4-40. Burlapping the seat.

Fig. 4-41. Burlapping the inside arm. Note solid wing frames.

Tack the burlap along the side rails being sure to bring it under the gut rails. Trim off any excess that isn't needed for the fold. Make the fold and tack the edge.

Next cover the inside back starting from the bottom rail. This is done in the same way as the seat.

The inside arms are started from the bottom of the gut rails and then up to the tops of the arms. Be sure you have two strips of webbing stretched across the arm from the gut rail to the arm top. This is needed to support the burlap and prevent it from being pushed in and torn loose. Tack the front of the burlap along the arm front and finish by tacking the burlap to the back. Figs. 4–41 and 4–42.

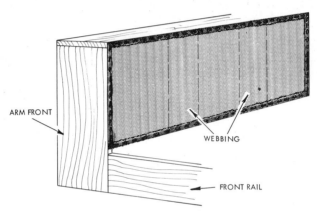

Fig. 4-42.   Inside arm with burlapping completed.

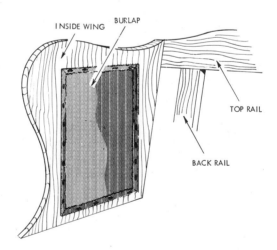

Fig. 4-43.   Padding and burlapping the inside wings.

Where the chair has wings the burlap is first tacked at the point where the wing is fastened to the arm and then stretched to the top of the wing and tacked. The sides are tacked last. In all cases the edge of the burlap is folded before the final tacking. Burlap is put on both sides of the wing. Fig. 4–43.

The outside arms are covered with burlap that starts at the edge of the top rail and goes down to the bottom of the bottom rail. The burlap is smoothed and tacked on all sides. In tacking to the side rails stop at the gut rail. This lower part is not tacked down because materials need to be brought through and fastened to the gut rails. The tacking is finished after all other materials have been fastened including the finish cover.

In most factories and many shops air pressure operated stapling guns are used to drive staples into the wood to hold burlap, cotton, muslin, and other fabrics to the frame. Because the frame is made of hard wood and heavy duty staples are required to take the strain of the fabric as well as to penetrate the wood only heavy duty machines can be used. Air operated are the most numerous but electric models are used. Some

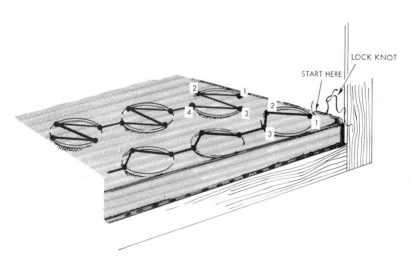

Fig. 4-44.   Sewing burlap to the springs.

of the very heavy duty hand operated spring types can be used but be sure that the staples are large enough to take the strain.

Staple guns have the advantage of being operated by one hand while the fabric is being smoothed and held by the other. They can be operated very rapidly and speed up work. However, be certain that any spring operated models will drive the staples into the hard wood.

SEWING BURLAP TO THE SPRINGS

The burlap is stitched to the springs either before or after the fox edging (Chapter 5) has been applied.

This is done in the same way that the springs were sewed to the webbing. The main difference is that you will have to use a curved needle and sew from the top. Placing the stitches and locking the thread are the same as when the springs were fastened to the webbing. Fig. 4–44.

QUESTIONS FOR STUDY

1. Why are springs tied?
2. In how many directions are the springs tied?
3. What is the reason for stretching webbing?
4. How tight should webbing be in the seat?
5. What method is used to fasten the springs to the webbing?
6. Why is it important to use lock knots on twine used with springs?
7. What is the edge wire?
8. Why is it used?
9. Why is webbing always folded before being finally. tacked?
10. Where are springs used in a chair?
11. Where is webbing used?
12. What purposes does the burlap serve?
13. How many openings are burlapped on a wing chair?
14. How many openings are burlapped on a Lawson style?

Stuffing and Padding

Chapter 5

Insiding includes the operations necessary to finish the inside surfaces of a chair or sofa. So far the work on the frame and springs has involved both inside and outside surfaces or parts of the furniture. Now just the inside areas will be worked on and the special requirements of them will be covered.

MATERIALS FOR STUFFING AND PADDING

All of the operations in upholstering have just one purpose. That is to provide comfortable furniture. While appearance and beauty are important they are secondary to the overall need for comfort. Since ancient times comfort and softness have meant almost the same thing in furniture. A comfortable chair has a great deal of softness in the seat, back, and arms combined with a firm springiness.

Early records indicate that softness was obtained by using dried grass as a stuffing for pillows and on chairs and sofas. Feathers and bird down were also used.

A major problem with the early types of stuffing and padding materials was their breakdown. Hay, moss, straw and similar materials dry out and become brittle with age and use. They break into small pieces and pack into hard masses. Feathers and bird down pack and mat into dense masses and need constant shaking and fluffing.

Modern upholstery became possible when methods of producing long lasting and non-shifting materials were developed. Among these were cotton sheets that were evenly packed. Curled hair is another product that found wide use. Curled hair is the durable coarse hair from hogs

Fig. 5-1. Foam padding is cut with electric knives in factories.

and cattle that has been twisted and treated so that a springy, long lasting material is formed. For many years these two materials furnished the basis for all fine upholstery stuffing.

Within the last few years modern chemistry has created new materials that have wide use in upholstering. Foam padding and cushioning materials have been developed that provide a maximum of softness with durability and ease of use. These have found new uses and broadened the field of upholstering. Fig. 5–1.

Foam rubber or foam plastic are now being made so that the deficiencies or problems of natural products are being overcome. Softness, size, and shape are under laboratory control. Coolness, light weight, ease of application, and flexibility of choice have been obtained.

Fig. 5-2.   Foam padding enlarged to show structure. Note pencil.

FOAM PADDING

Foam padding is manufactured from either natural rubber or synthetic plastic in controlled densities so that soft, medium, or firm cushioning is obtained. The density is controlled by the amount of air whipped into the mixture.

The foam materials are made of blends of ingredients in liquid form. This liquid is beaten or whipped until a foamy mass is made. When the foam reaches the right thickness it is poured into molds and heat treated to set the foam permanently. The result is a sponge-like mass that is largely air bubbles. In some forms additional openings are made in the center to provide greater softness and additional ventilation. Fig. 5–2.

The various combinations of air bubbles, holes, or cores in the molds, the thickness of the slab of foam, and the stiffness of the materials provides a wide range of choice in selecting foam padding. Fig. 5–3.

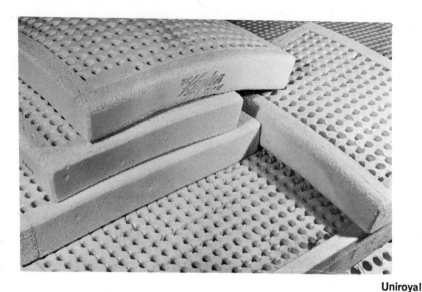

Fig. 5-3.   Foam padding comes in many sizes.

Manufacturers control the ingredients that are added to the foam so special qualities can be provided when necessary. Foams can be made that have resistance to weather, oil, water, abrasion, impact, tearing, low temperatures, stains, fires, and other hazards. These qualities are in addition to the normal resistance of the foam to them. All foams are normally tested for softness, aging, deflection, and ordinary low temperatures. As a result foam padding and stuffing have an indefinite life in upholstery as the problems of earlier, somewhat similar materials have been overcome.

When foam is used as padding over springs the controlled size, uniformity of thickness, and ease of application speed up the work by reducing padding to one operation instead of the several required by other methods. If foam cushions are used instead of the ones made of springs and padding even greater savings in time can be made as stuffing a cushion becomes one simple operation instead of many needed

Fig. 5-4.　Some of the shapes of foam cushions available.

by other methods. Many standard sizes of cushion fillers are available so that selection is quite easy. Fig. 5–4.

Odd shapes such as T cushions can be made by cutting the shape from a large slab or by joining smaller pieces to form the needed stuffing. Foam is joined by using rubber cement according to directions on the cement. Tapes can be cemented to foam padding to provide fastening surfaces to hold it in place. Cutting of foam is done with a sharp knife. Cuts are made from both sides if the piece is thick. Thinner pieces can be cut with large scissors.

While foam padding has provided great savings in time and labor in the upholstering field there are times when the preference is for the traditional methods of stuffing and padding with curled hair and cotton. The details of this method are covered.

APPLYING FOX EDGING

When you have applied burlap to all the inside openings, the next operation is to place fox edging (roll edging) along the edge wire wherever weight will be placed on the edge. In an arm chair the fox edging would only be used across the front. On an end unit of a sectional sofa the edging would go across the front and around the open side. On a center unit of a sectional the edging would go all around the springs except at the back. The purpose of the edging is to protect the covering from a sharp bend over the edge wire and cushion it.

Buy commercial fox or roll edging for this operation. Cut it the same length as the edge wire it is to cover. Lay out your upholstery pins and a large curved needle threaded with #252 twine. Also have a small curved needle handy as you will need it later.

The fox edging has a burlap strip along one side. This is placed on top of the burlap covering the springs so that the rolled part of the edging is centered over the edge wire. The edging should extend out and up from the wire. When you have centered the edging over the edge wire, pin the flat part of the edging to the burlap covering on the springs.

Now take the large curved needle threaded with #252 twine and push it through the back of the burlap strip of the edging as close to the edge wire as possible at one end of the edging. Make a loop around the edging and fasten it with a lock knot, pulling the thread tight. This can be done at either end of the edging but right-handed people generally find it more convenient if the first loop is placed at the right side as you face the chair. Cut the thread. Now go to the opposite side and make a similar loop and lock knot. Fig. 5–5.

Go to the right corner of the springs and put the needle through the burlap strip of the edge roll as close to the rolled part and the edge wire as possible. Be sure to bring the needle out through the burlap on the front of the springs as close to the edge wire as you can. Make a lock knot to securely fasten the edge roll and the edge wire together. Now make another stitch about 1½ inches from the first loop. Fig. 5–5. Before drawing the needle all the way through the burlap wrap the thread

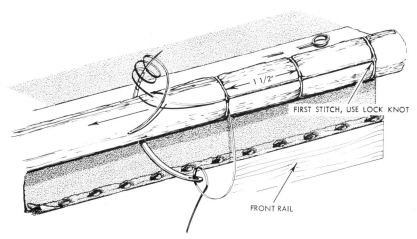

FIRST STITCH, USE LOCK KNOT

FRONT RAIL

1 1/2"

Fig. 5-5.   Applying fox edging to a seat.

around the needle loosely two or three times. Then draw the thread as tight as possible. Fig. 5–5. This locks the thread. Repeat this stitching all the way across the spring. At the other end make two additional knots for safety. Be sure the stitches are tight and close to the edge wire so the fox edging will not work down off the wire.

When the edging has been firmly stitched to the edge wire you sew the flat part of the edging or lip to the burlap on the springs.

This lip should be stitched as tight as the roll part of the edging. Use the small curved needle for this and the #252 twine. Start with a lock knot and make the stitches about a half inch long. Lock each stitch with a twist knot. Space the stitches about every inch. Fig. 5–6.

When the edging has to be carried around a corner you will have to make a miter. This is done by measuring to the corner. Mark on the outside of the rolled part. Cut a V-shaped piece out of the lip with the point of the V at the mark on the edging. Cut into the padding in the rolled part and remove some of the padding being sure not to cut through the front of the edging. Bend the edging around the corner and check to see that the edging comes together snugly with no opening or

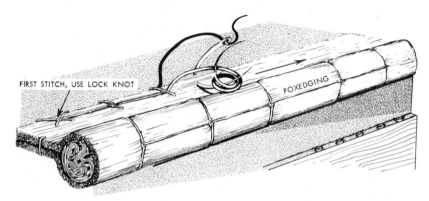

Fig. 5-6.   Sewing fox edging in place.

bunching. Try making the cut slightly smaller than you think it should be. You can always take a little more off but too large a cut will be difficult to fix.

Once the corner has been cut to fit the edging is sewed to the burlap.

Sometimes ready-made edging is not wanted. Then a hand-made edge is used. This is made by lightly sewing a strip of burlap about six inches wide to the seat with about four inches extending over the edge. Padding such as curled hair or burlap, is put inside and the burlap rolled into a tight edge and sewed in place. Filling the burlap evenly and tightly requires time and experience so the hand-made edge is rarely used.

PADDING WITH CURLED HAIR

Curled hair, or hog's hair as it is sometimes called in the trade, is a mixture of hair from cattle, horses, and hogs. The hair is cleaned, sterilized, and twisted into ropes. The ropes are treated so that the hair becomes permanently curled when it is removed from them. The shape of the hairs prevent them from packing tightly or matting so they give a bouncy or springy foundation. Curled hair is generally used loose on seats and backs and in cushions and is held in place by stitching. Curled hair may also be coated with liquid rubber and molded into sheets. This is termed rubberized hair and is used where loose hair would not stay in place as on arm tops or where a sharp edge is needed. The rubberized hair can be cut into shapes and used where there are problems in padding. Wherever curled hair is used it should be covered by a layer of cotton or foam rubber. This is because the ends of some of the hairs may work through the covering and become a nuisance.

Curled hair is sold by the pound. Some of the average amounts needed are: seat, one lb; inside arm, one-half to three-quarters lb per arm; back, one lb; and one-half lb for each wing.

The hair must be distributed evenly to avoid lumps and unevenness in the finished padding. To do this you slowly pick the hair away from a mass in your hand, letting it fall on the place where you want it. You will have to be sure to go over the entire surface so that the hair is evenly distributed. It will appear quite high and loose but it will settle after being sewed in place.

In applying hair padding to the seat deck take three-fourths of a lb of the hair and apply it to the seat on top of the burlap covering the springs. Stay back about five inches from the fox edging. Fig. 5–7.

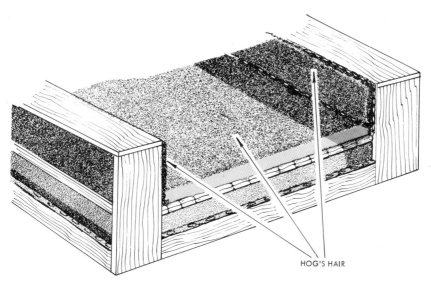

HOG'S HAIR

Fig. 5-7. Curled hog hair being applied to pad a seat.

The other one-fourth lb of hair needed for the seat is applied to the five inches in back of the fox edging and to the front of the seat between the fox edging and the front rail.

To apply curled hair to the front seat it is necessary to tilt the chair so the hair will fall on a flat surface. When the hair has been applied evenly it is stitched and the chair is turned to another position so the rest of the hair can be put on. The inside arms, and the inside wings are frequently padded with hair and the chair must be laid on a side to do one side and then laid on the other side to do the other.

When the hair has been evenly appied to an area, stitch it in place. To do this you will need a large or medium curved needle and #252 twine. Take a length of twine about 8 ft long. Start at one side of the seat, the right is best for most people, and push the needle through the hair and burlap so the full width of the needle goes under the burlap before it comes back up. Make a lock knot. The needle is pushed through from front toward back of the seat and the knot is made in the center of the stitch. Fig. 5–8.

Next move the needle to the left about 2½-3 inches and make another

Fig. 5-8.   Stitching curled hair in place.

stitch. Wrap the twine around the needle to make a twist knot. Center the knot in the stitch and pull it reasonably firm. Repeat this stitch all the way across the seat. Make another row two or three inches from the first one. Keep on making these stitches until the entire bottom is covered and the curled hair is held in place loosely but securely. Fig. 5–8.

If the hair has been applied properly it will be springy but not so loose that it shifts or comes out.

Where rubberized hair is needed as on the arms of square styles of furniture the sheet of hair is cut the same size as the surface it is to cover. This gives a flat padding with square edges. The rubberized hair retains its shape but is not quite as springy as the loose hair. Pads of rubberized hair are held in place by tacking through the bottom edge to the frame. Use small tacks and drive them at an angle along the side. This is similar to the toe-nailing used by carpenters.

Some upholsterers used pads of rubberized hair over the springs to save time. The pads are stitched to the burlap along the edges.

Foam rubber is used to replace rubberized hair in many padding operations. In using foam padding always remember to have a layer of cotton between the foam and any metal surfaces so that the foam is prevented from rubbing on the metal. Foam is held in place in the same way as rubberized hair, by lightly tacking the lower edge to the frame. This is shown in Fig. 5–13.

COTTON PADDING AND MUSLIN COVERING

The final padding is usually a layer of cotton placed over curled hair or foam rubber. The cotton is covered with the final fabric or a sheet of muslin. While the final fabric can be placed directly over the cotton a better job usually can be done when muslin is used first. There are two reasons for this. One is that the padding can be adjusted through muslin rather easily. The second is that it is easier to learn the various steps of measuring, cutting, sewing, tacking, and finishing on some material that can be thrown away in case of error without wasting a great deal of money.

In practically all procedures the final fabric is applied in exactly the same way as the muslin. The same directions apply as well to one as the other. Consequently following the directions for covering with muslin gives practice in applying the final fabric.

The first step after the curled hair has been stitched in place is to measure the chair or sofa in order to cut the muslin to the right size.

Measure the width first. This measurement is taken across the seat and down to the side rails passing under the gut rails. Add two inches to this figure for error, folding, and tacking. Measure the depth from the front of the seat to the back and down to the back rail. Deduct three inches to allow for the front seat.

Find the center of the muslin by folding it in half and mark the center with a crayon or a small cut. Place the center of the muslin on the center line of the seat and about five inches back from the fox edging. Bring each side of the muslin down to the side rail passing under the gut rail. Pull down firmly but not so hard as to pull down the springs in any way. Tack with 4 oz tacks at the front only. Be sure to fold over an inch of muslin to tack through.

Take a small curved needle and thread it with #252 thread, just a little more than the width of the seat. Stitch through the muslin and lock knot it around the edge wire at end. Then use small stitches, about a half inch long and an inch apart, to sew the muslin to the burlap on the chair seat just about five inches in back of the fox edging. Fig. 5–9 shows the muslin in place. Lock the twine at the opposite side with two or three loop knots.

The muslin is tacked to the side rails at each side and sewed to the burlap across the seat about five inches from the edge. Now bring the muslin to the front of the chair so it hangs over the edge of the seat. Place a layer of cotton over the seat so it extends down each side and three or four inches are shoved under each gut rail. Pull the cotton to the back and shove about four inches under the bottom rail. Take the muslin and put it over the cotton all the way to the side rails and the back rail. Shove the muslin under the gut rails and the bottom rail. Cut a slit in the muslin where it goes around the upright back rail.

Pull the muslin at one corner until it is smooth and tight. Then stay tack it to the back rail. Pull the other corner until it is smooth and tight and tack it, also with a 4 oz tack. Figs. 5–10 and 5–11.

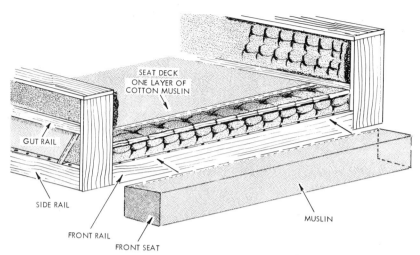

Fig. 5-9.　Square arm chair with muslin on seat.

Fig. 5-10.　Fastening muslin at back of seat.

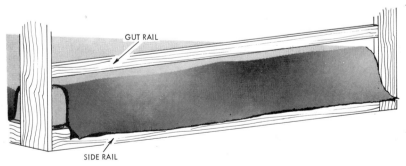

Fig. 5-11.　Fastening muslin at side of seat.

For the front seat cover measure from the edge of the seat deck muslin on one side forward to the edge of the fox edging. Measure along the fox edging on the front of the seat to the other side and then measure back to the deck muslin. This gives you the width of the muslin for the front seat. Next measure in the center of the seat from the seat deck muslin to the fox edging and then down to the front rail. Add about an inch and you have the depth of the muslin.

Lay the muslin so it is centered on the seat. Pull the edges down under the gut rails to the side rails. Use a crayon to mark along each edge wire next to the arms. Mark a straight line from the front edge wire to the edge of the muslin. Allow about a half inch on the lines for seams and cut off the rest. Sew the muslin together where you cut out the square section so that it forms a box-like covering. Fig. 5–12.

Put the stitched muslin cover on the front of the seat. Fold the back

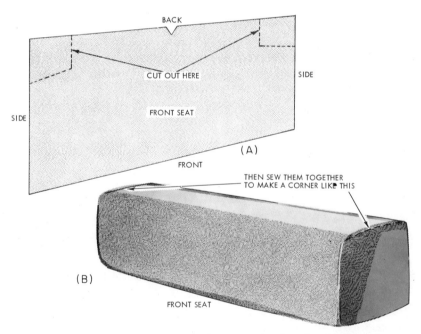

Fig. 5-12. Cutting and sewing muslin for the front seat.

edge over to give a fold about an inch wide. Pull this fold under the gut rail and to the side rail at each side. Stay tack it. Be sure the muslin is tight and smooth and the corner seams are in the right place before finally tacking it down. Now stitch the muslin to the burlap on the front seat next to the muslin covering the seat deck.

Place a piece of cotton the width of the seat on it so that it comes down to the top of the front rail. Bring the muslin down over it and tack each corner so the cover is tight and smooth over the cotton. Make sure the cotton does not get onto the front rail, just to the top of it.

Check the height of the corners after they have been stay tacked. Be sure they are the same height. This should be done by measuring from the bottom of the front rail to the top of the spring corner. Adjust any differences by shifting small amounts of cotton. Finish tacking the muslin to the front rail. Be sure to start at the center and work toward each side smoothing out any wrinkles that may be there.

When you reach the corner cut the muslin carefully with a pair of scissors up to the top of the front rail. This will permit you to pull the side of the muslin under the gut rail so that it can be tacked on the side rail. The finishing fabric will be applied in this same way.

UPHOLSTERING A SQUARE ARM

The arms are upholstered by padding with hair and cotton and then covered with muslin in preparation for the final cover. So far the square arm has had burlap applied on the inside and curled hair has been stitched to it.

Now pad the top of the arm by cutting rubberized hair or foam padding to the exact size of the arm top. Tack this to the frame with 4 oz tacks placed along the sides of the padding and tacked into the frame at a slight angle. This toenail type of tacking avoids making dents in the top of the padding. Fig. 5–13.

Next place a layer of cotton over the padding so that one piece goes from the gut rail on the inside over the arm top and down to the gut rail on the outside, and from the front of the arm to the back frame. Allow about a half inch of cotton to stick out past the frame on the front of the arm. Tuck about two inches of cotton under the gut rail on the

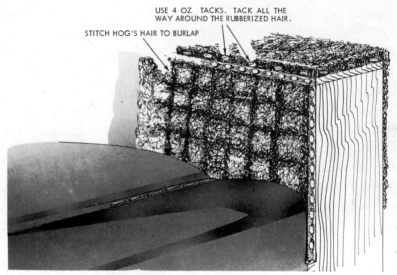

USE 4 OZ TACKS. TACK ALL THE WAY AROUND THE RUBBERIZED HAIR.

STITCH HOG'S HAIR TO BURLAP

Fig. 5-13. Padding the side and arm with curled hair.

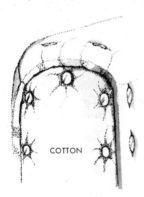

COTTON

Fig. 5-14. Cotton padding is placed on arm.

inside of the arm. Tack the cotton to the frame on the front on both sides. Pull the cotton to the back and tuck it between the inside arm and the back rail. Tack to the sides of the back rail. Use 4 oz tacks.

Cut cotton to the exact size of the arm front and tack it to the arm front. The cotton covering the top and sides of the arm will extend over the cotton on the face of the arm. The arm is now completely covered with cotton. Fig. 5–14.

Make muslin covers for the arms to hold the cotton in place and to give a smooth surface for the final covering. To make a cover first measure the arms. Measure the width from the front of the arm to the back of the frame and add two inches for seams. Measure the depth from the bottom of the side rail to the top of the arm and add two inches. Make two pieces this size for each cover. There is so little difference between the inside arm and the outside that one set of measurements will do for both.

Now measure across the top of the arm. Add one inch. Measure

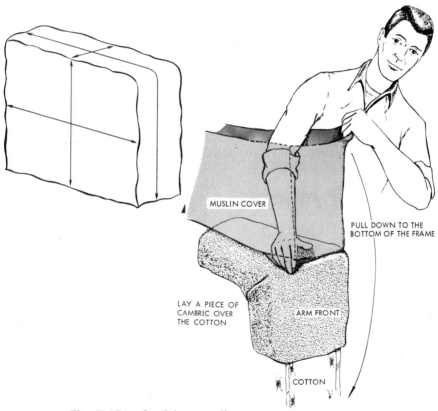

Fig. 5-15.   Applying muslin cover on square arm.

along the top of the arm from the back to the front and then down to the bottom of the front rail. This will give a piece that is a few inches wide and several feet long. Make all measurements on the frame itself and not on the padding. This will insure a snug fit that will hold the padding in place.

Sew the three pieces together so they form a cover. When you finish the cover will have the seams on the outside and keep it this way for the time being.

Lay a piece of cambric over the cotton at the front corner of the arm. This will prevent the cotton from bunching up when the muslin is put on. Fig. 5–15.

Take the cover and lay it along the top of the arm. Make sure the cover is even on the front. Stay tack the cover at the back at the top of the arm. Cut a slit in the cover if it is needed to pass the back upright rail.

Put your arm inside the cover from the top. Fig. 5–15. Push the cover down so that it fits snugly on the arm. Use one hand to hold the cover firmly on top of the arm and pull the rest of the cover down to the bottom of the front arm. When you pull the cover down you will turn it inside out and the seams will be on the inside. Stay tack the cover at the bottom of the arm front.

Remove the stay tacks at the back and stretch the muslin. Cut it where it goes past the bottom rail and also at the front rail. Tack the muslin along the back rail. Push the muslin on the inside of the arm down between the inside arm and the seat. Tack it to the gut rail. Tack the muslin on the outside arm along the back upright rail but be sure to leave the bottom open as it is necessary to get inside in future operations.

UPHOLSTERING ROUND ARMS

The details of padding and covering a round arm style differ from the square arm because you do not have flat surfaces to work with. The padding and covering have to be rounded to conform to the frame.

To get roundness and proper depth the arm front has welt applied around the front. Fig. 5–16. This is similar to using fox edging on the

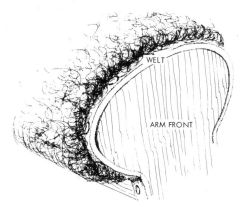

Fig. 5-16.   Placing hair padding on a round arm.

seat. The welt is made from strips of burlap about two inches wide and several feet long. A piece of welting cord is placed inside the burlap and the burlap is drawn tightly against the cord and then tacked to the frame so that about a $\frac{1}{4}$ inch of the welt sticks out in front of the frame. Start the welt at the bottom of the arm next to the tacking rail on the outside. Then carry the welt around the arm, tacking it every two inches, to the bottom of the arm at the front rail. Fig. 5–16.

The inside arm should be webbed, burlapped, and padded as described previously. The hair padding should be stitched in place. Now apply curled hair to the top of the arm. This hair cannot be sewed to anything so the cotton will have to hold it in place. When there is sufficient padding to pad the arm, cover it with cotton. To do this cut a piece of cotton that is a few inches wider than the arm. Measure from the tacking rail around the arm and down to the bottom of the gut rail. Allow two or three inches extra.

Lay the cotton gently on the curled hair so that about a half inch hangs out over the welt. If the arm has a backward slope or curve in it, as a provincial style, shape the cotton to fit. Tack the cotton in place all along the welt.

Place the muslin over the cotton so that it completely covers all of the cotton with enough over for tacking. Allow two to three inches to hang over the front of the arm. Stay tack the muslin at the tack rail at the very front. Pull the muslin along the inside of the arm and stay tack it just above the front rail. Remove the stay tacks at the tack rail and re-stretch the muslin, pulling it as tight as you can. Tack it permanently. Do the same with the stay tacks on the inside arm. Pull the muslin to the back of the arm and make V cuts at the upright and bottom rails.

A V cut is made to give finished edges where any fabric goes past a rail. Pull the cloth to the rail and fold back the part that goes past it. Cut from the edge of the folded piece toward the center of the rail. About 1½ in. from the rail make a cut to one corner and another to the other. Fold under the V-shape tongue. Pull the fabric around the rail and fold under the edges. Tack firmly. Fig. 5-17.

Stretch the muslin along the outside of the arm and at the back. This shapes the arm. Tack. Pull the muslin on the inside at the top and back. Tack. Keep stretching and tacking along the back and gut rails. Finish tacking the outside arm along the tack rail.

Tack the muslin to the arm front so it is tight and without wrinkles. Make four or five pleats where the muslin goes around the curve of the arm. Fig. 5-17. This is done by stretching the muslin tight and

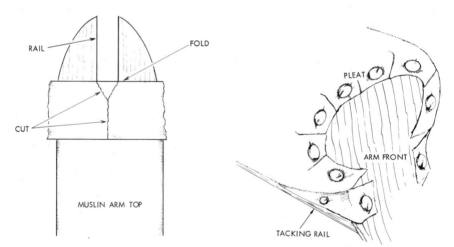

Fig. 5-17. Placing muslin cover on a round arm chair.

carefully folding the extra material underneath. Be sure to tack through the pleats to keep them flat.

This same method can be used on square arms if you do not wish to make a fitted cover as described in the preceding section. With square arms only one pleat is needed at each corner or two for each arm.

Remember that the procedure in applying the muslin is identical with that used in applying the finish fabric except that at the very bottom of the chair where the muslin is fastened to the gut rail and the finish fabric is tacked to the bottom of the bottom rail.

THE INSIDE WINGS

Wings are found on early American and provincial styles of furniture. In some of these the wings serve as head rests while in others they are entirely ornamental. The wings are prominent features of a chair and should be well done and comfortable. Because of the curved shape of the wings they require a little more care than many parts of the chair.

Wings may be solid or open depending on the size and the manufacturer of the frame. Where the wing has an open center in the frame a strip of webbing should be applied. This is stretched just tight enough to keep the burlap and padding from being pushed in or sagging. Use 4 oz tacks for fastening the webbing.

Burlap is fastened over the opening. Remember to double the edge of the burlap before tacking.

Pad the wing with curled hair. Use an even layer over the burlap. Generally about a half pound of hair is sufficient except for very large styles. This is stitched to the burlap and tacked to the frame outside the burlap. If the wing is solid wood it is best to cut a piece of rubberized hair the exact size of the wing and tack it to the wood. Add a layer of curled hair and stitch it to the rubberized hair. Fig. 5–18.

The curled hair is covered with one or two layers of cotton that is trimmed even with the outside edge of the frame. The cotton is tacked with 4 oz tacks about every two inches around the edge of the frame. The inside wing consists of the inside surface and the edge of the wood frame. The cotton, muslin, and finish fabric are carried over the edge of the wood frame to the outside corner. The cotton padding stops at

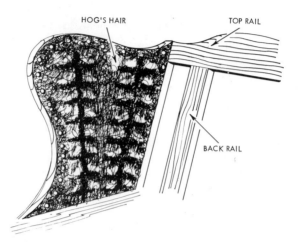

HOG'S HAIR   TOP RAIL

BACK RAIL

Fig. 5-18.   Placing hair padding on a wing.

the outside edge but the muslin and cover are tacked to the frame on the outside of the frame and right next to the edge of it. Remember that the padding and coverings for the wings starts at the back or outside of the wing and goes around to the back of the back upright rail.

In measuring for the inside wing always include the edge of the frame and then add two inches to the measurements for tacking.

The illustration in Fig. 5–19 shows the places where measurements are taken for the cotton padding. The muslin and finish fabric go just about two inches onto the back of the frame for tacking. These tacks are covered by the outsiding. Cut two pieces of muslin this size.

Center the muslin on the wing. Fold under an inch along the bottom of the wing and tack with 4 oz tacks from the front to the back. Be sure to get the muslin tight.

Next stretch the muslin along the back of the wing and tack it. Make a cut in the muslin where it goes around the top rail. Follow the muslin around the top of the wing pulling it tight and tacking it to the outside of the frame. You may need to make several small pleats in the curved parts of the wing to get a smooth fit. Finish tacking it all around.

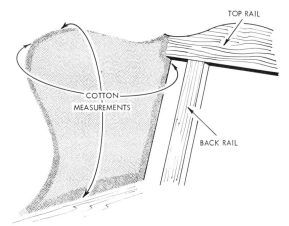

Fig. 5-19.   Cotton padding covers hair padding on wing.

Check the wing by running your hand over the tacked muslin. It
should be tight and smooth. If not, untack and do it over.

There is a tendency for some upholsterers to slight the wings and
just place a layer of cotton on them and then cover with the fabric. This
is a questionable practice as the wings are such a conspicuous part of
the chair that any lack of quality may be quite noticeable.

UPHOLSTERING A PLAIN OR LAWSON BACK

The back is one of the most comfortable areas of upholstered furniture so it is important that it be done right. It also receives hard use and
must be constructed with that in mind.

Cover the springs, which have been sewed to the webbing and tied
with an 8- or 16-way tie, with a layer of burlap. If the springs are the
Marshall unit type enclosed in muslin put on the burlap too as the muslin may not prevent the padding from sifting through and you will need
the burlap as a foundation for fastening the padding. Tack the burlap
to the edge of the frame on all sides and then sew it to the springs in the

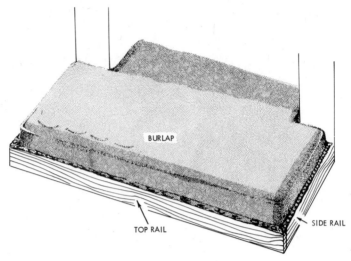

Fig. 5-20. Burlapping an inside back.

same way as the seat springs were. Fig. 5–20. It is not necessary to sew to each spring in a Marshall unit but only to enough places in the unit to keep the burlap from sagging or getting out of place.

Next apply one to one and a quarter pounds of curled hair on the burlap making sure to pick it carefully and scatter it evenly over the entire area of the burlap. Sew the hair to the burlap. Fig. 5–21.

Another method is to use a sheet of one inch medium soft rubberized hair. This is cut to fit the exact shape of the inside back and stitched to the burlap around the edges. A thin layer of curled hair is placed on top of the rubberized pad and stitched to it.

Regardless of the method of padding used a layer of cotton is put on over the hair padding. Measure the back in both directions and allow about two inches extra in each direction. Be sure the cotton extends down to the gut rail at the back. Tack the cotton in place.

Measure the muslin in the same way as the cotton making sure that you have allowance for folding and tacking. Center the muslin and

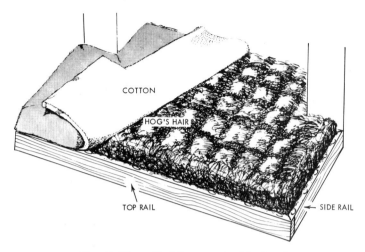

Fig. 5-21.   Padding an inside back.

make sure that it is flat. Stay tack the bottom first to the gut rail. Pull the muslin tight and stay tack to the top rail. Set the chair upright.

There are two styles of plain backs. One, described above, has the inside back meeting the outside back. The other has the inside and outside back separated by a flat area several inches wide that runs from the top of one arm, up and across the back and down to the opposite arm. This is covered by the back band. Remember to pad this area the same as the rest of the back. That is, use a thin layer of rubberized hair and then add a 2 in. deep layer of curled hair, follow with the cotton padding and then the muslin. Tack the rubberized hair to the frame and stitch the curled hair to it.

Pull the muslin back and make cuts where it meets the inside arm and the arm top. Shove the muslin past the inside arm and pull it out to the back rail. Stay tack it to the outside of the back rail. Fold the top corners so they are flat and smooth. If all of the surface is snug and smooth finish tacking all around. Fig. 5–22.

While tacking has been mentioned in connection with fastening the

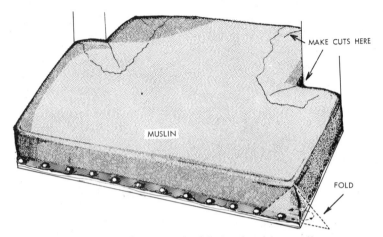

MAKE CUTS HERE

MUSLIN

FOLD

Fig. 5-22. Covering inside back with muslin.

Duo-Fast Fastener Corp.

Fig. 5-23. Pneumatic stapler fastening seat cover.

muslin, staples are used a great deal where volume production requires fast methods. Because of the hard wood used in furniture only power operated staplers and large staples that will take a great deal of pull can be used. Either air or electric powered staplers are in use. A few of the heavy duty hand operated models may be suitable but be sure to test them before using. Fig. 5–23.

OTHER METHODS OF PADDING

The detailed instructions have covered the widespread method of using curled hair and cotton for padding. While this has been the commonest method of padding there are several others that have been important.

Spanish moss is the springy inside fibers of the moss-like plant that hangs from the trees in the far south. The moss is cured by a wetting and drying process to remove the soft outer part and leave only the tough center strand of fiber. Moss is handled in the same way as curled hair.

Other fibers have been used some such as sisal and kapok. In a few cases feathers and bird down were used. These are used very little at the present time.

Rubberized hair which is curled hair treated with liquid rubber and then formed into pads is used frequently in addition to the loose hair where there is difficulty in holding and shaping the loose material. It can be used to replace the loose material on seats, cushions, arms, and other places. The rubberized hair is more expensive than the loose and is generally thought to be less springy. However, there is saving in time in applying it compared with picking and stitching loose hair.

Foam padding has been the greatest change in padding upholstered furniture in history. Foam, which may be either rubber or plastic, is extremely soft and has advantages in applying that make it superior to most of the other materials in some way.

Foams come in a wide range of thickness, size, shape, and can be manufactured to meet special needs such as exposure to cold temperatures, abrasion, chemicals, and similar hazards. Many standard sizes of padding and cushions are made and require a minimum of hand work to use. Sharp knives or scissors can be used to shape foam padding although power saws with special blades are used in places where a large volume of foam padding is used. Fig. 5–1 shows a special saw in use. Foams can also be shaped by cementing pieces together with rubber or plastic cement.

Muslin is almost always applied over cotton padding to keep it in place and prevent lumping. This is not necessary with foam padding but covering with muslin is suggested as a standard practice in order to gain familiarity with cutting and measuring the various shapes needed. Covering with muslin is recommended to prevent some fabrics from rubbing on the foam and causing wear. Also muslin covered furniture can have new outer fabric applied without disturbing the padding.

It has been mentioned that foam padding should be protected by muslin to prevent the cover from rubbing on the foam and causing it to crumble. In upholstered furniture covering the foam padding with a layer of Dacron, Kodel fibers, or cotton is strongly recommended also to protect the foam from heat and rubbing and to make a softer padding.

QUESTIONS FOR STUDY

1. Where should the fox edging be placed?
2. What is the purpose of the fox edging?
3. Why is curled hog hair used as a padding?
4. How does rubberized hair differ from loose?
5. Where is rubberized hair used, and why?
6. How much loose curled hair is used on a seat?
7. How is the loose curled hair kept in place?
8. Is a muslin cover necessary over the cotton? Explain.
9. Why is muslin used in upholstering?
10. Where is foam padding used?
11. What advantages are claimed for foam padding?
12. Are there other materials for padding furniture? Name one.

Chapter 6

Making the Cushion

CUTTING AND SHAPING CUSHIONS

The procedure for making a cushion is the same for any cushion regardless of size or shape. Once you understand the basic method the differences are slight. Fig. 6–1.

In making a cushion it is essential that you make it firm. At first it may seem too firm or too thick, but after some use it will flatten down and assume the shape of the chair. Unless the packing is quite firm in

Kroehler Mfg. Co.

Fig. 6-1. Stuffing a cushion in a factory. Note unfilled covers at left.

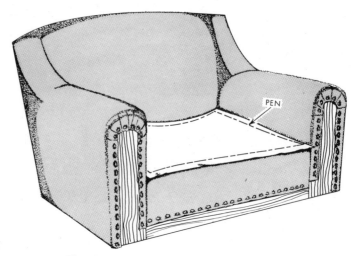

Fig. 6-2.   Measuring for the cushion.

the beginning the cushion may soften too much, the cover will wrinkle, and the stuffing shift and become lumpy.

The first step is to measure the width of the seat between the inside arms. Then measure the depth of the seat which is the distance along the inside arm from the farthest point at the corner at the inside back to the front. Fig. 6–2.

Allow 3 inches more for seams and working edge on both width and depth.

Now cut two pieces of muslin to these measurements.

The cushion will need to be fitted to the curve of the back. This is done by laying the muslin on the seat deck and carefully smoothing it over the entire seat. Take a felt pen or a soft pencil and with the tips of your fingers push it hard against the inside back and the inside arms. Move the marker along so a mark of the exact shape of the back and arms is made on the muslin. Be sure to go into the back corners as far as you can. Fig. 6–2.

For the beginner it is best to mark each piece of muslin separately

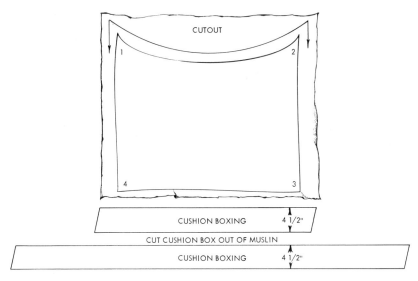

Fig. 6-3. Cutting diagram for a cushion.

and to cut them separately. Cut the muslin around the lines leaving about a quarter inch extra on all sides for a seam. Fig. 6–3.

Now measure the distance around the outside of the cushion. You can use a tape measure to obtain the outside size of the muslin cover. This will give you the length of the cushion boxing (or edge). Cut several pieces of muslin 4½ inches wide so that they will be the total length of the distance around the cushion. It is not necessary to have this in one piece but allow for any seams.

Start in the center of the back and sew the boxing to one of the large pieces. When you have finished sewing the entire edge sew the boxing together where it joins at the back. Cut off the excess.

Now take the muslin with the boxing sewed to it and lay it flat on a table. Fold the boxing down on top of the other piece so that it lies flat. At the front corner carefully fold the boxing at a 45° angle. Make a small notch at the tip of the fold. Fig. 6–4. This notch is the place where

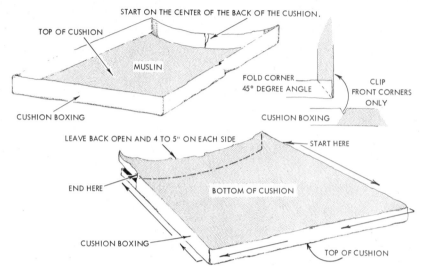

START ON THE CENTER OF THE BACK OF THE CUSHION.

TOP OF CUSHION

MUSLIN

FOLD CORNER
45° DEGREE ANGLE

CLIP
FRONT CORNERS
ONLY

CUSHION BOXING

CUSHION BOXING

LEAVE BACK OPEN AND 4 TO 5" ON EACH SIDE

START HERE

END HERE

BOTTOM OF CUSHION

CUSHION BOXING

TOP OF CUSHION

Fig. 6-4. Sewing diagram for a cushion.

the corner of the other side of the cushion will come. Pin the corner of the other side to this notch.

In sewing the second side of the cushion to the boxing start about five inches in front of the back corner and sew around to a similar distance on the other side. This will leave the back open so that the stuffing can be placed in the cushion. When the muslin has been sewed turn it inside out. This will put the raw seams on the inside.

FILLING THE CUSHION

If possible you should fill the cushion on a cushion machine. However, if one is not available you can use other methods of filling the cushion.

First lay out a strip of cotton that is the width of the cushion and twice as long with about three inches over. Lay this on a table or the cushion machine so that a part just the size of the cushion is on the table, let the rest hang over the edge.

Place another layer of cotton the exact size of the cushion on top of this. Scatter about ¾ of a pound of curled hair evenly on top of the layers of cotton. This should give a layer of picked hair about two inches deep.

Next place a cushion spring unit on top of the picked hair. (If the springs of the cushion unit are not completely enclosed by muslin or burlap place a piece of burlap the exact size of the spring unit on each side of the springs and stitch loosely to the outside springs or fasten with hog rings. This prevents the hair from falling between the springs.) Add another layer of hair of the same depth as the bottom layer. Add a second layer of cotton the same size as the cushion.

Make three or four rolls of cotton. Cut about a foot strip from the full width of the cotton and roll it into a tight roll. Make three or four of these rolls so that they will go completely around the spring unit. Place them next to the springs and then bring the front piece of cotton

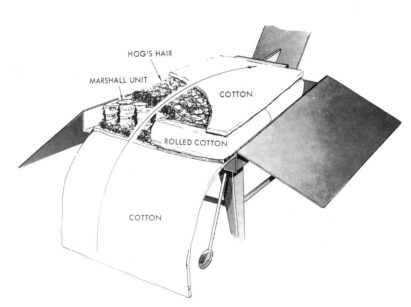

Fig. 6-5.　Filling for the cushion.

up and over the entire mound of cotton, hair, and springs so that a smooth front is made. Be sure that the outer layer of cotton goes to the back of the cushion. Fig. 6–5.

If you are using a cushion filling machine you close the machine by bringing the sides down and locking them. Operate the machine so that the cushion is compressed to about three inches less than it was. Figs. 6–6 and 6–7.

Place a small wad of cotton in each of the front corners of your muslin cover. Slip the cover over the sleeves of the machine. Open the machine slightly so the cover is stretched snugly but not tight.

Operate the cushion machine so that the padding is pushed out of the

Fig. 6-6. Cushion filling machine, hand operated.

Fig. 6-7.   Cushion filling machine in open position.

sleeve and into the muslin cover. On many machines this is done by pumping a foot lever.

If a cushion filling machine is not available a simple one can be made by using two pieces of sheet metal bent into V shapes. These are slid over the filling and drawn together by a strong rope until the cover can be slipped over. Then the filling is pushed out into the cover. Hand fillers are available that have hooks and hand holes for efficient operation. Fig. 6–8.

The back seam of the cover is sewed shut with a curved needle and twine.

If only an occasional cushion is being made the cover can be put on entirely by hand. This is done by placing the cover on a flat surface. The top cover is sewed to the boxing only at the front. The filling is done inside the cover. The bottom cover and the boxing are filled with

Fig. 6-8. A hand unit for filling cushions.

the cotton, hair and springs. When all the stuffing materials are in place the top cover is pulled back and pinned to the boxing at the back. The side and back seams are then sewed by hand with a curved needle and twine. The seams should be pinned first so that any unevenness of the padding can be adjusted before sewing.

The fabric cover is put on in the same way except that an additional layer of cotton is added on the top and bottom sides of the cushion. The fabric cover is made with a covered welt along the seams and blind sewing is employed for the final seams. See Chapter 8 for details of blind sewing.

FOAM CUSHIONS

Foam cushioning has become one of the biggest fields in furniture manufacturing. Usually referred as foam rubber, the foam may be either a rubber or a urethane plastic material. The foam is made by whipping the liquid rubber or plastic and then pouring it into molds for forming and curing. When cured the material consists of an elastic, spongy mass that holds its shape.

Various densities of foam rubber are produced by controlling the amount of air whipped into the liquid. Thicknesses from 1 inch to 5 inches are made. Many standard sizes are produced so that the filling for a cushion may often be obtained ready for use. In other instances slabs can be cut and cemented together to produce any size or shape wanted. See Fig. 6–9.

Some types of foam are made with cores or openings that run most or all the way through the material. The type with many small cores, often called pin-core, is especially good for upholstery as it provides a breathing action in addition to its cushioning.

In measuring for foam cushions allow an inch more in both width and depth to the size of the cover for the size of the cushion. This will keep the cover tight and firm. When filling the cushion with foam no machine or device is needed. The foam is folded in half and inserted in the cover and then opened.

What is said to be an improved method of using foam cushions is

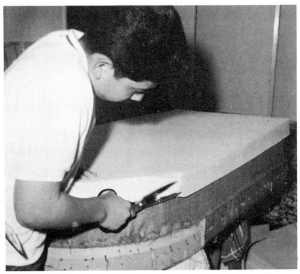

Fig. 6-9.   Cutting foam padding for a cushion.

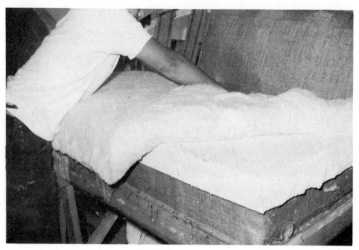

Fig. 6-10.   Placing foam padding and filling in a cushion.

to wrap the foam material with a layer of Kodel, Dacron, or cotton. This gives a softer cushion and helps protect the foam from heat and moisture. In a tight seat (cushions are not removable) two layers of cotton are recommended over the foam cushion. Fig. 6–10.

In filling the cushion make sure that the flaps of the raw seam all go downward. This will make the welt run straight.

SEWING IN A ZIPPER

There is an idea that it is very difficult to sew a zipper into a cushion. Actually it is a simple process and one that is easily learned.

The zipper is put in the fabric cover to give a better appearance and fit. It is not intended to be used for removing the cover for cleaning. All parts of upholstered furniture should be cleaned together so that there will be no color change. The zipper merely saves time in putting the finished cover on the cushion and in making it possible to reach inside and straighten the cushion and cover.

After you have cut out the top and bottom of the cover measure across

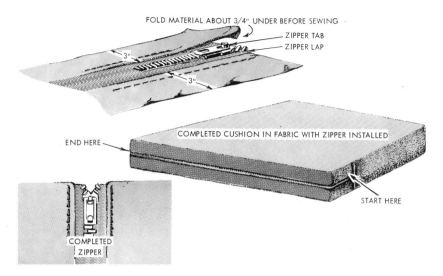

FOLD MATERIAL ABOUT 3/4" UNDER BEFORE SEWING

ZIPPER TAB

ZIPPER LAP

3"

3"

END HERE

COMPLETED CUSHION IN FABRIC WITH ZIPPER INSTALLED

START HERE

COMPLETED ZIPPER

Fig. 6-11.   Installing a zipper.

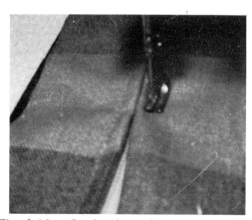

Fig. 6-12.   Sewing in a zipper on a cushion.

the back and about six inches on each side. Cut two strips of material this size and three inches across. Fold back about ¾ of an inch along one edge of each strip and sew it down. Lay the two strips with the folded edges butting and the face of the fabric up and place the zipper under them so that the sewing lip of the zipper is on the underside. Sew the zipper to the folded edges. This will make the zipper almost invisible when it is closed. Fig. 6–11.

Sew the fabric with the zipper in it to the top and bottom covers in place of the boxing at the back and about 5 inches on each side. Insert the cushion through the zipper and zip shut.

It is important that the zipper be long enough to go completely across the back and several inches on each side so the opening will be large enough to insert the cushion. Fig. 6–12.

Zippers can be inserted on slip covers in this same way.

QUESTIONS FOR STUDY

1. Why must a cushion be made extra firm?
2. Name the layers of materials in a built-up cushion.
3. What is used to give firmness to the edge?
4. Why is cotton placed in the front corners of the muslin cover?
5. What purpose does a zipper perform?
6. How much allowance should be made for a foam filling?
7. What is the best type of foam cushion filling?

Handling the Fabric

Chapter 7

SELECTING FABRICS

One of the most important decisions in upholstering is the selection of a fabric or material to cover the outside. This is quite a problem as there are about 5000 different kinds of patterns, prints, colors, and weaves. One manufacturer of vinyl upholstery material offers more than 500 textures, patterns, and colors in this one material.

Inevitably the beginner will be tempted to buy the cheapest material because it is his first attempt. This is a defeatist attitude as it implies a lack of confidence in his ability to learn how to complete a first-class project.

This is one of the main reasons why the instructions have always stressed completing the work in muslin. In many cases muslin can be left out and the final fabric applied directly over the padding. However, muslin does give a better piece of furniture as the padding can be adjusted more easily through it than through a heavy fabric. Muslin also gives a smooth surface for applying the fabric or covering material. Learning the proper methods of cutting and fitting with muslin is easier and less expensive than with fabrics. Then, too, fabric is harder to work with, in most cases, and a neat looking cover is harder to achieve without practice.

In selecting fabrics for the final cover there are several general points to keep in mind. First, is that the finished chair or sofa is going to be placed in a room with other furniture and the color and pattern of the chair must be in harmony with the rest of the furnishings. Second, are the conditions which the furniture will be subjected to such as hard usage, likelihood of getting dirty or soiled, expected life, pets, and whether a slip cover will be used. If children and pets will be around the furniture then ease of cleaning and scuff resistance may be important. Furniture used in a recreation room should be able to take hard use and be resistant to stains from food and beverages.

The quality of a particular fabric can be checked in several simple ways. One way is to feel the fabric. If it feels hard or seems to be heavily starched it should be avoided. Squeeze the fabric tightly when you have it in your hand. If wrinkles stay in it when you open your hand it is likely to be poor quality. Good materials will unfold and lay flat with almost no wrinkles.

Hold the material up to a strong light or the sun. If a lot of light can be seen through it the weave is loose and will not wear well.

For the beginning upholsterer the best material should have a small figure or an over-all pattern. This simplifies cutting and permits using more of the material as there is no wastage in matching such as occurs with a large pattern. Large prints and stripes need to be matched on the various parts of the furniture for best effect.

Some of the standard fabrics that are widely used on furniture are Matelasse, Brocatelle, Frieze, Velvet, Chromespun, rayon, nylon, rayon and cotton, and viscose and acetate mixtures.

Vinyl plastic is one of the widely used covering materials for upholstery. It is extremely wear resistant and cleaning is done by washing with soap and water. Airplane and bus seats, office and theatre seats, automobile seats, and hotel furniture are a few of the many places where vinyl has become standard as a covering material.

Naugahyde was one of the original vinyl covering materials. It has a woven fabric back that allows it to be sewed like any fabric and that gives greater pliability. Naugahyde is available in 34 different patterns, as many as 65 colors in some patterns, for a selection of more than 500 colors and patterns. Fig. 7–1.

The fabric-backed vinyl is handled in the same way as cloth fabric. It is tacked to the frame or blind sewed. Seams and welt are sewed on standard machines using upholsterer's thread and a large stitch. Vinyl has an additional advantage as it can be molded around curved surfaces by being heated. This is described later.

Fig. 7-1.   Naugahyde covered furniture.

Materials for covering upholstered furniture should be obtained from an upholstery supply house or a dealer that specializes in upholstery materials. Be sure to avoid slip cover and drapery fabrics as these are not made for furniture covering and do not hold up when used for this purpose.

MEASURING AND LAYOUT

Some people seem to think that in measuring furniture you simply take a tape measure or a ruler and mark down the measurements as you make them.

Measuring should be done so that you have accurate figures to use for laying out the various materials and for cutting. To avoid mistakes follow exact steps in measuring and use the same steps every time.

Always measure the width first. This is standard in a great many fields and serves to avoid confusion. In upholstery it is important as the fabric comes in 54 inch widths and the design or pattern must run correctly across the width. If this is done there will be no mistakes in the pattern when the work is completed. This automatically avoids many errors.

Always measure across the widest part of a surface. If there is enough material to cover this there will be plenty for the rest.

List the parts of the project in sequence and then measure them in that order. This will prevent overlooking any part of the work. In making measurements always remember to add about three to four inches to all measurements where stretching and tacking will be done, and about a half inch to each one where there will be a seam.

The following order has been found to be a practical one and if you learn to use it you will be sure to have all the measurements you will need.

	Abbrev.	Name		Abbrev.	Name
1.	S	Front seat	7.	O.A.	Outside arms
2.	B.B.	Bottom band	8.	O.B.	Outside back
3.	I.A.	Inside arm	9.	F	Flounce
3A.	A.T.	Arm top	10.	P	Panels
4.	I.B.	Inside back	11.	Ch	Cushion
4A.	B	Back band	12.	C.B.	Cushion boxing
5.	I.W.	Inside wings	13.	Z.B.	Zipper boxing
6.	O.W.	Outside wings	14.	W	Welt

Note: Numbers refer to Figs. 7–2 and 7–3.

Once you have made the measurements list them by name and then show the width and depth. Also mark down the number of pieces of that size you will need. For example, you will need two pieces for the inside arm. Other items that require two pieces include inside wings, outside wings, outside arms, panels, and cushion.

You will need several pieces for cushion boxing, zipper boxing, welt, and the flounce. Only one piece will be needed for bottom band, front seat, inside back, outside back, and back band.

In measuring be sure that you run the tape measure or ruler all the way to the back of each piece. Fig. 7–2. Also be sure to look over the

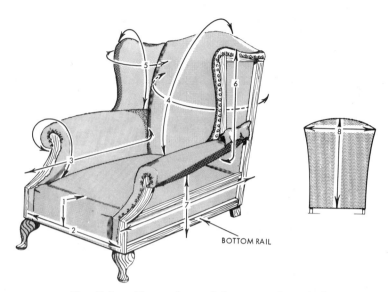

Fig. 7-2.   Measuring points on a wing chair.

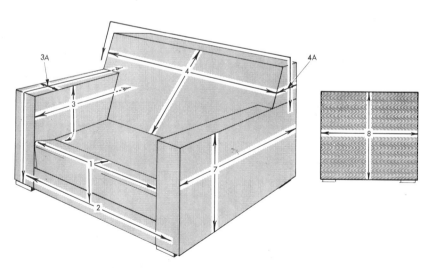

Fig. 7-3.   Measuring points on a square arm chair.

illustrations (Figs. 7–2 and 7–3) and see just where the measurements should be made. For example the front seat will need to have five inches added at each side in order to make the corners and finish the seat. Notice that certain lines are carried around some parts in order to include the entire amount of covering needed. This is done on the inside wings, the inside arms, the back, and the front seat. Also be sure that the tape measure or ruler is all the way it can go at the places where one part overlaps another as in the back corner where the inside arm, inside back, and cushion meet.

The importance of measuring the widest point is shown in Fig. 7–3. Unless the fabric is cut to cover the widest place an unsightly seam will be needed to piece on to it or another piece will have to be cut.

The same sequence of measuring is used for sofas as well as chairs. With sofas there will be two or three cushions and right or left backs or even a center back. Be sure to allow for the extra number of pieces and mark them as left, right, or center in your list.

MASTER CUTTING PLAN

The cutting plan is one of the most helpful of all the diagrams in the book. With it you can be sure of making all of the parts you will need and you will also have a guide for buying the right amount of material.

The simplest way is to make a listing as shown in the upper left corner of Fig. 7–4. The three columns are for the number of pieces needed, the name of the part, and the size. Next take a large sheet of paper and lay out the pieces. You can do this by making a scale drawing. If you use a 1/16 scale every 1/16 space on a ruler will be equal to one inch. Measure off three and 6/16 inches for the 54 inch width of the material.

List the parts you have measured in the list. Start with the widest pieces first. If there are any that are 54 inches wide start with them and draw a line at the proper scale for each piece. Label with the proper abbreviation.

Next take pieces that will go in the width evenly, say those that are 27 inches wide and mark them on your plan.

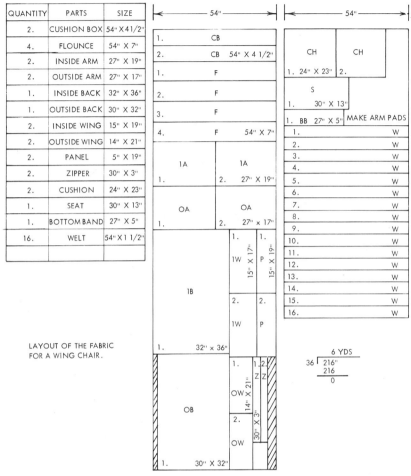

QUANTITY	PARTS	SIZE
2.	CUSHION BOX	54" X 4 1/2"
4.	FLOUNCE	54" X 7"
2.	INSIDE ARM	27" X 19"
2.	OUTSIDE ARM	27" X 17"
1.	INSIDE BACK	32" X 36"
1.	OUTSIDE BACK	30" X 32"
2.	INSIDE WING	15" X 19"
2.	OUTSIDE WING	14" X 21"
2.	PANEL	5" X 19"
2.	ZIPPER	30" X 3"
2.	CUSHION	24" X 23"
1.	SEAT	30" X 13"
1.	BOTTOM BAND	27" X 5"
16.	WELT	54" X 1 1/2"

LAYOUT OF THE FABRIC
FOR A WING CHAIR.

Fig. 7-4. Master cutting plan. Wing style shown.

Be sure that the width is always marked down first and measured across the layout. Continue to put in the pieces as you would a jig saw puzzle. When you have laid out all the pieces, then add up the depths of all the pieces that are on the left side of the plan. Divide this figure by 36 to obtain the number of yards of material needed.

① 10 yds   ② 10 yds   ③ 10 yds   ④ 10 yds   ⑤ 10 yds

⑪ 10 1/2 yds   ⑫ 6 yds   ⑬ 10 yds   ⑭ 7 yds   ⑮ 10 yds

㉑ 7 yds   ㉒ 7 1/2 yds   ㉓ 6 yds   ㉔ 9 yds   ㉕ 6 yds

㉛ 4 yds   ㉜ 5 yds   ㉝ 6 yds   ㉞ 6 yds   ㉟ 6 yds

㊶ 5 1/2 yds   ㊷ 5 yds   ㊸ 6 1/2 yds   ㊹ 5 yds   ㊺ 6 yds

㊿ 4 1/2 yds   52 3 1/2 yds   53 4 yds   54 4 yds   55 4 1/2 yds

Uniroyal

Fig. 7-5.   Furniture styles and amounts of fabric for cover.

(6) 10 yds (7) 10 yds (8) 10 yds (9) 12 yds (10) 12 yds

(16) 9 yds (17) 10 yds (18) 11 1/2 yds (19) 10 1/2 yds (20) 4 1/2 yds

(26) 5 1/2 yds (27) 5 yds (28) 3 yds (29) 2 1/2 yds (30) 2 1/2 yds

(36) 5 yds (37) 5 yds (38) 5 yds (39) 5 yds (40) 5 yds

(46) 6 yds (47) 6 yds (48) 6 yds (49) 5 1/2 yds (50) 5 1/2 yds

(56) 5 yds (57) 6 yds (38) 5 1/2 yds (59) 4 yds (60) 5 yds

Uniroyal

Fig. 7-5. (cont.)   Furniture styles and amounts of fabric for cover.

Check your measurements carefully to avoid overlooking a piece. When you have obtained the fabric lay it out on a long table or work bench, face down. Use clean paper to cover the top of the bench.

With a yard stick and a sharpened piece of chalk mark the fabric. Start with the widest pieces as you did on the list you made. When you have drawn in the lines of the parts that need to be full width, then add the others, remembering that the width of the piece runs across the 54 inch width of the fabric. As each piece is marked on the fabric with chalk lines be sure to mark the name or abbreviation of the piece on it. Now use a sharp pair of large scissors to cut along the lines. As each piece is cut off lay it carefully on a pile. Be sure that you reverse the pieces so that the outside of the material faces another outside. This prevents the chalk marks from getting on the face of the material where they will have to be cleaned off. Keep pairs of parts together is a further precaution against mistakes.

By drawing the pieces to scale on a sheet of paper first you can see how much of the fabric will be left and be able to move some of the parts around so that a minimum of material is wasted.

However, do not skimp on the measurements in order to save a few inches of material. Parts that are cut skimpy so that there is not enough allowance for tacking or sewing will have to be stretched too much in being applied. The edges may pull loose and a poor job is the result.

After you have measured the material needed check the amount shown in Fig. 7–5. Be sure to select the style that matches your project and allow for any extras, such as flounce, that may not be shown. Number 34 in Fig. 7–5, with a flounce added, matches the chair used for the dimensions shown in the cutting layout Fig. 7–4.

MAKING AND APPLYING WELT

In applying the finish fabric there are many places where welt is used. The purpose of the welt is to give a finished look to seams and edges. There is no structural advantage in using welt; it is purely decorative.

Most furniture has the welt made of the same fabric as the cover. However, in some cases the welt may be made of a contrasting color for a striking effect. This would be a matter of personal taste. The welt is sometimes called piping or cording as it is made of a cord covered in fabric.

Welt is made of strips of material about $1\frac{1}{2}$ inches wide when a cord of $\frac{5}{32}$ inch diameter is used. If a thicker cord is used then the width of the material would have to be increased accordingly.

Some people feel that welt should be made from scrap material. This may result in having a great many seams in the welt and difficulty sometimes in finding long enough pieces to give a good appearance across the front of cushions and arms. There is also a good chance of not having enough fabric unless provision is made for it in laying out the fabric. Normally about 14 strips of welt should be laid out across the full 54 inch width of the fabric.

When the fabric for the welt has been cut it is sewed into one long strip. This is done by laying a piece at right angles to another piece with the front of the fabrics facing. The strips are sewed across the corner at a 45° angle. Fig. 7–6A, Fig. 7–7. When this is opened you will have a flat seam that runs across the material at an angle. When you have joined the fabric together the welt cord is sewed in.

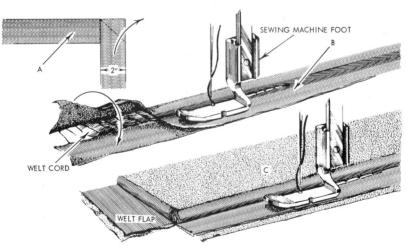

Fig. 7-6. Sewing welt.

Fig. 7-7.   Sewing welt diagonally across corner.

The cord is sewed in by using a welting or cording foot on a sewing machine. This foot runs very close to the needle and makes a tight seam. The fabric is folded over the cord so the edges are even. Then this is sewed as close to the cord as possible so that a tight covering is made. Fig. 7–6B. Follow directions from the sewing machine manufacturer for the proper use of the cording foot. The part of the welt away from the cord is called the flap. This is used for fastening the welt in place either by sewing to the fabric or by tacking to the frame. It is important that the flap be placed correctly when sewing so the welt will be in the right place.

In sewing welt to other parts of the furniture it is important that the corners be made square. This is done by sewing right up to the corner. Cut straight through the flap right up to the cord first. Lift up the sewing machine foot and turn the entire piece and let the foot down again. This should produce the correct corner. Fig. 7-6C.

Remember in sewing the welt to the fabric that the welt is placed on the face of the fabric and so the flap faces the outside and is about even with the edge of the material. This will give a good half inch seam when it is sewed and opened. Where the welt is sewed between two pieces of material such as a cushion top and side boxing, it is easier to sew the welt to the top and then to sew the boxing to this rather than to sew them at the same time although this is usually done by skilled workers in the industry. Fig. 7–9.

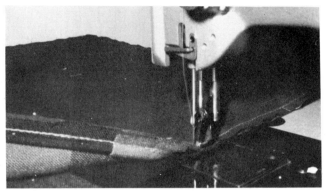

Fig. 7-8.   Sewing boxing and welt to the inside back.

Fig. 7-9.   Welting the front seat.

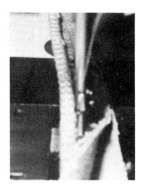

SEWING BOXING TO OTHER AREAS

In sewing a cushion, arm cover, an inside back, or an ottoman cover, the steps are identical.

The best way is to first sew the welt, as discussed previously, to the larger piece of the fabric.

Then this piece is turned over so the finished side is facing down and the back is up.

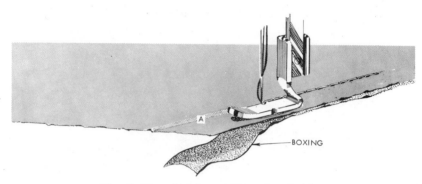

Fig. 7-10. Cutting and sewing boxing.

Then the boxing or other part of the cover is laid on the machine, face up, with the larger piece being placed on it, face down. The pieces are sewed together. By having the piece with the welt sewed to it on the top you accomplish two things. First, you will have a smoother cover as there will be less pulling of the fabric. Second, you will have the seam of the welt and fabric up so that you can work close to it and make a finer seam than if you were unable to see the first seam.

The steps to be remembered are: Sew the welt to the cover first. Sew the boxing to the welt and cover second. Fig. 7–10.

FINISHING THE FRONT SEAT AND SEAT

The front seat is finished in the same way as the muslin cover. The fabric is measured for the full width of the seat and then 5 inches are added on each side. The depth is measured from 5 inches in back of the fox edging to 2 inches below the bottom rail. The corners are cut out and sewed to form a box. Fig. 7–11.

A piece of welt about a yard long is taken and centered on the fabric

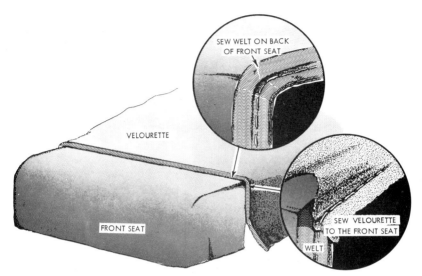

SEW WELT ON BACK
OF FRONT SEAT

VELOURETTE

FRONT SEAT

SEW VELOURETTE
TO THE FRONT SEAT

WELT

Fig. 7-11.   Finishing the front seat.

box. The welt is sewed to the fabric across the back edge and about 2 inches down each side.

Next a square yard of pulling or upholstery denim (sometimes called velourette) is centered on the front seat. This is turned over on the fabric and welt and all three pieces sewed together.

Then the fabric is pulled over the muslin. The ends of the welt are taken and pulled down between the seat and the inside arms to the bottom rails. Stretch the welt and tack the ends to the rails. This should give a straight line of welt across the seat. With the denim pulled forward use a curved needle and #252 twine to sew the flat part of the seam joining the denim, welt, and fabric to the seat. Be sure the needle goes into the burlap and not just the muslin. Lock the twine at each end.

Now place a layer of cotton over the muslin on the seat and then pull the denim over it. Tack the denim to the back and bottom rails as you did the muslin.

Finish fastening the fabric to the front and gut rails. This is the same as with the muslin.

QUESTIONS FOR STUDY

1. Which measurement should be made first, width or depth? Why?
2. What two quick tests can you make on a fabric to tell quality?
3. Why is muslin useful in upholstering?
4. Where should measurements be made on a seat or cushion?
5. A cutting plan helps in several ways. Name two.
6. What is welt? Where is it used? What does it do?
7. Describe briefly the procedure in sewing on boxing.
8. What is the width of the front seat?

Finishing the Outside

Chapter 8

Outsiding covers the work done on the outside surfaces of upholstered furniture to complete and give a finished appearance to the whole operation of upholstering. There are a number of procedures included in the field of outsiding some of which require care and patience as neatness and proper fit are essential.

In upholstery factories there is a definite job title that covers this work. It is the responsibility of the man doing the outsiding to make sure that the furniture is finished when he completes his part. Fig. 8-1.

The techniques used in outsiding are designed to give a finished appearance and to add some decorative details as well. The outsiding conceals the raw seams, tacked areas, frame, and details of the work done on the inside. The inside work is brought to the outside of the frame for tacking or stapling. The outsiding covers only this and provides a smooth, finished look to the entire chair or sofa. Decorative details such as a flounce, panels, buttons, gimp, and decorative tacks may be added in some styles. Legs may need to be attached if they were not done as part of the frame.

There is a definite order to the outsiding operations. It is outside wings, outside arms, outside back, panels, flounce, and the bottom cambric.

Before proceeding to finish the outside there are two methods of fastening fabrics, blind sewing and blind tacking, that should be learned as they are important in giving a professional finished look to the work. These methods are used to fasten the fabric in such a way

Fig. 8-1. Blind sewing and tacking on an outside back.

that no tacks, staples, or stitches show on the outside of the finished furniture. Both are simple but require some practice to obtain skill. Study these two methods and practice them on some left over material until you know how they are done. For example, try making a blind seam with white thread on black fabric. If the thread shows you need more practice.

BLIND SEWING

Blind sewing is a technique that is used in several places in upholstering such as on the sides of the outside back, the outside wings,

124 *Upholstery: Refinishing and Restyling*

the outside arms, the cushion, and the front panels when they are built up with padding. It can be used in several other applications in upholstering too. The objective of blind sewing is to join two finished surfaces together so that no seam shows.

For blind sewing you will need a medium size curved needle and some heavy carpet thread or nylon thread. Cut the thread about twice the length of the part you are going to sew.

Start at a corner that is most convenient for you. This is usually the upper right corner of the back for right-handed people and the upper left corner for left-handed people. Otherwise you will be twisting your wrist awkwardly. Allow plenty of time and avoid rushing the operation.

Push the needle through the welt and the outside fabric of the side cover. Pull the needle out completely and lock the thread.

Turn the needle on its side and push it through the fabric of the side cover right along the welt. Make the stitch about a half inch long. Pull the needle out completely. Take the needle and push it through the welt as close to the place where it came out the side cover as you can. Keep pushing the needle around the corner, through the welt and out through the back cover. Pull the needle out completely. Next make a stitch along the fold of the outside back. Pull the needle out completely and then go through the welt again. Keep the thread tight and continue all along the fold. Fig. 8–2.

In blind sewing there are two points to keep in mind. One is to keep the thread along the inside of the folds of the fabric to avoid puckering and the other is to go straight through the fabric and the welt to the other side. Be sure to keep the thread in a straight line at all times and to pull it tight. This will pull the folded edge of the fabric up close and slightly underneath the welt. No thread shows if the sewing is done correctly. Be sure all three pieces, the two covers and the welt, are sewed together. Lock the thread at the start and the finish.

One of the tricks of achieving a successful blind stitch is to be absolutely sure you are sewing on the inside of the folds whether they are on the outside back, boxing, or the outside arm. Otherwise the fabric will not be pulled up to and under the welt. Another is to keep the stitches straight where they go through the welt and into the other fold. If you

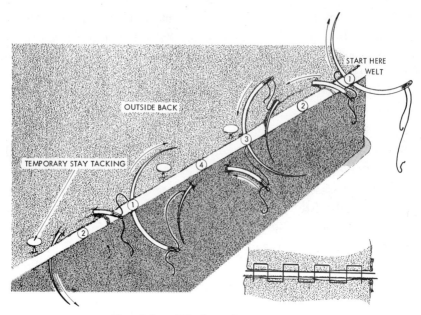

START HERE
WELT
OUTSIDE BACK
TEMPORARY STAY TACKING

Fig. 8-2.   Blind sewing procedure.

always make a practice of putting the needle back into the same hole where it came through the fabric and to the back of the thread you will avoid difficulties.

In blind sewing there should be no thread on top of the fabric when the stitch is completed. The thread goes along the inside of the fold, out through the edge of the fold, into the flap of the welt and on into the edge of the fold on the other part of the chair. The needle is turned with the curve parallel to the fabric when the stitch is made inside the fold. Then it is turned 90° and pushed straight through the welt into the other fold. In order to turn the needle you have to pull it out of the fabric but be sure to put it back without leaving a loop of thread on top of the fabric. When you push the needle through the fold bring the point out as close to the fold as you can. Start the next stitch along the fold from the same opening in the fabric made by the thread.

BLIND TACKING

Blind tacking is used for the same purpose as blind sewing. That is to create a finished covering without any signs of tacks or staples. It is used in places where blind sewing cannot be done as along the edges of exposed wood.

There are two kinds of blind tacking used in upholstery work. Both use cardboard strips and tacks but the ways in which the two are applied differ. For convenience these two methods are designated as blind tacking and tack strip application.

In blind tacking the fabric is carefully laid out on the surface it is to cover. About three quarters of an inch is folded under where it is to be tacked. Stay tack the fabric that is folded under. Open the folded fabric and place a cardboard strip right along the fold. Tack the strip to the frame with 12 oz tacks about every two inches. When the fabric is pulled tight over the cardboard strip it will have a sharp edge and will cover the cardboard strip and tacks. Fig. 8–3.

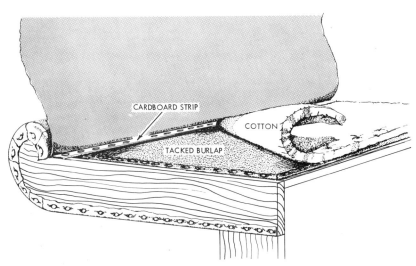

Fig. 8-3. Blind tacking an outside arm.

Where there is a slight curve the cardboard strip can be bent slightly to go around the curve. On larger curves small slits can be cut part way through the cardboard strip and it can be bent to fit around the curve. (Fig. 8–5.)

A tack strip is a strip of cardboard that has large tacks fastened in it about every two inches. The tacks are held in place and are backed up by another strip of cardboard.

TACK STRIPS

Tack strips give the same effect as blind tacking but they can be used in unusual situations. They can also be used to replace blind sewing for finishing outside backs and similar places where the fastening must be concealed. Tack strips are very useful for fastening some materials, such as plastic, leather, and other coverings, that are difficult to sew.

In applying the tack strip first place the fabric in position and stay tack it in place. Cut a length of the tack strip to go along one side of the cover. If there is a welt place the tack strip on the outside of the welt with the tacks pointing up. Fig. 8–4.

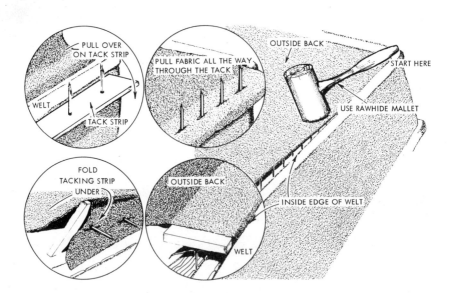

Fig. 8-4.   Blind tacking using a tack strip.

Take the fabric and pull it up and over the tacks. Bring the fabric down making sure that the tacks penetrate the fabric. Be careful as the tacks are sharp and painful injuries can occur.

When the entire length of the tack strip has been inserted through the cover lift the strip up and turn it under so the tacks are pointing down. This should bring the tack strip right along the inside of the welt. Fig. 8–4.

Use a rubber mallet or a rawhide upholstery mallet to drive the tacks into the frame as you go along. Hold the tack strip in place with one hand and then drive the tacks in with the mallet in the other hand. After the entire strip has been tacked go over it with the mallet again and pound the tacks in firmly.

THE OUTSIDE WING

The outside wings are quite conspicuous and the work on them should be carefully done so that a good appearance is the result. To do this the first step is to trim the entire front edge of the outside wing with welt. Start at the bottom of a wing below the arm, Fig. 8–5, and run it along the edge of the wing to the back. Do not cut the welt here but continue to run it along the top of the outside back and over to the opposite wing. Bring it along the outside edge of the wing and down to the opposite arm. Use 4 oz tacks to fasten the welt to the frame.

Now cover the opening in the wing with a piece of burlap. (Some wings are one piece of wood so this step may be omitted in that case.) Cut the burlap large enough to cover the opening with enough over to provide a double tacking edge on all sides. Stretch the burlap as tight as possible when tacking it. Fig. 8–5.

Next lay the finishing fabric face up on the wing. Mark the exact shape of the wing by drawing a piece of chalk along the edge. Cut the fabric about an inch outside of this mark to give an area for tacking. Stay tack the fabric as close as possible to the welt folding the tacking edge under. Use 4 oz tacks about every four inches.

You will need some cardboard strips about a half inch wide. Place a strip on the folded part of the fabric and as close to the welt as you can get it. Start at the bottom of the wing on the front edge and tack

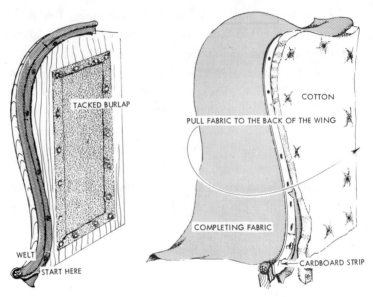

Fig. 8-5. Finishing procedure on an outside wing.

through the strip to the frame with 10 oz tacks spaced about every two inches. Stop the tacking strip at the top of the wing where it starts to go toward the back.

Pad the wing with a layer of cotton so that it comes right up to the welt. Hold in place with 4 oz tacks.

Pull the cover fabric back over the cotton to the frame at the back. Stay tack the fabric in place with the fold as close to the welt as you can get it. Be sure to fold all excess material under and make the folds straight and as close to the welt as possible.

Do not finish fastening the top, back, and bottom sides of the fabric now. Just stay tack them. These will be blind sewed to the inside wing, back cover, and outside arm later on. Do both wings in the same way.

THE OUTSIDE ARM

The outside arm is one area that is occasionally skimped in finishing upholstered furniture. It is a visible area and needs to be neat looking, however, it receives no strain or wear and there is a tendency to just fasten the fabric so it looks neat without doing anything else. Some upholsterers just cover the opening in the frame with cardboard or burlap and apply the cover.

To do the best job one layer of padding should be placed on the outside arm. This will give a rounded, full appearance that is similar to the appearance of the other surfaces. Without the padding the cover will look flat and sag after a time.

First, cover the opening in the frame with burlap stretched as tight as possible. Remember to tack through a double layer. Fig. 8–6.

Cut the finishing fabric so there is about two inches overlapping the frame. Fold under about three quarters of an inch and place the fold right up to the inside arm. Fig. 8–6. Stay tack at the front and back of the arms.

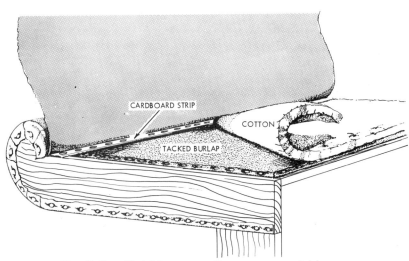

Fig. 8-6. Finishing operations on an outside arm.

Blind tack the top of the outside arm by tacking a cardboard strip on the inside of the folded material as close to the inside arm as possible. Be sure to smooth the fabric before tacking. Use 12 oz tacks and space about every two inches.

Pad the outside arm by placing a layer of cotton over the entire area. Allow about a half inch to overhang the front. Keep the cotton about the same distance in front of the back frame. If you are planning to use a flounce keep the cotton about two inches above the bottom of the bottom rail so you will have a smooth surface for fastening the flounce. Tack the cotton in place with 4 oz tacks.

Now pull the fabric down over the cotton and tack it to the bottom of the side rail. Be sure to stretch the fabric at one corner and stay tack it and then stretch the other corner and stay tack it. Then complete tacking the entire bottom. Next tack the front of the cover along the front edge of the arm and then stretch the cover to the back and tack to the back of the upright back rail.

In square arm styles the cover may be applied in this way or it may

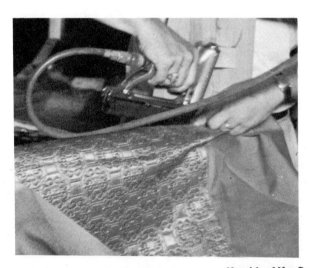

Kroehler Mfg. Co.

Fig. 8-7.   Sofa arm being stapled with power stapler.

be made in the shape of a square sided bag and then pulled down over the muslin and tacked at the bottom. The cover fabric is applied in the same way as the muslin and directions for making the cover were contained in the section on upholstering a square arm chair.

Power equipment is used in factories to simplify the work and save time. The employee shown in Fig. 8–7 is using one hand to smooth the fabric and the other to operate a pneumatic staple gun. There is no lost time in putting tacks on a hammer.

THE OUTSIDE BACK — CURVED OR WING STYLES

The back of the furniture may be unseen against a wall or it may be the most conspicuous part if the furniture is placed out in a room. Chairs are always being moved and the back should be treated the same as the rest of the surfaces.

In any case cover the opening in the frame with burlap stretched tight and tacked all around the edge. Use 4 oz tacks through a double thickness of burlap.

Measure the fabric by laying it on the back and marking the exact shape of the curved areas on the fabric with a sharp piece of chalk. Cut to this shape with about three quarters to an inch extra allowed for fastening.

Fold the extra material under. Start at the top and place the folded edge as close to the welt as possible. Stay tack to the frame. Lift the cover up or throw it over to the front of the chair so you can get at the folded part. Place a cardboard tacking strip on the top of the curve, bending it slightly to follow the curve. Put some 12 oz tacks in it near the top. Then place a few at one side of the curve. Next place a few on the other side of the curve. Keep tacking a few tacks on each side so that the fabric is tacked down evenly. Stretch the fabric tight as you place the tacks. Keep the tacks right up against the welt. When the top has been completely tacked bring the fabric down and check for tightness and smoothness.

Cover the back with a layer of cotton. Keep the cotton about a half inch from the sides so you can complete the edge. Tack the cotton in place with 4 oz tacks.

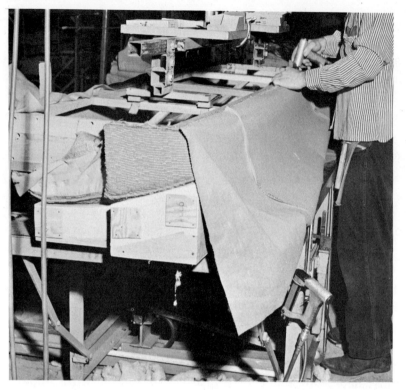

Fig. 8-8.   Sofa back being fastened with pneumatic stapler.

Now pull the fabric down over the cotton and stretch it as tight as possible. Tack it to the bottom of the bottom rail.

Fold the fabric along the edges and stay tack or pin so that you have smooth edges against the welt. Blind sew or blind tack when you have finished pinning the edges. Blind sewing is better on a curved back as the stitches can follow the contour better than a straight piece of cardboard. Sew through the welt to the back of the outside wings and the back of the outside arms along both sides. Be sure to read the instructions on blind sewing again.

In factories long staples are driven in by power staplers to hold fabric in place. Only heavy duty staplers that can drive into hard wood can be used. Staplers permit smoothing the fabric with one hand and stapling it with the other. Fig. 8–8.

THE OUTSIDE BACK — SQUARE STYLE

The outside back on a square style is somewhat easier to complete than on a curved style. Otherwise there is very little difference.

On a square back style cover the opening in the frame with burlap stretched tight and tacked around the edge. Now start at the bottom of the frame on the right side and apply welt to the frame so it extends about a quarter inch beyond the wood. Tack the welt at a bottom corner and stretch it to the top corner along the side. Tack it at the top. This will give a straight line. Now tack all along the side. Use 4 oz tacks and space about every two inches. Next stretch the welt across the top and fasten it in the same way as you did the side. Then do the other side.

Place a layer of cotton over the burlap and up to within a half inch

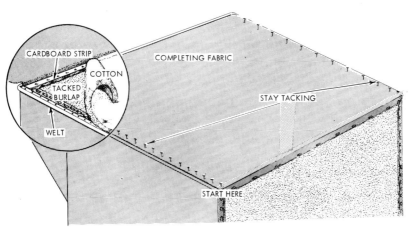

Fig. 8-9.   Completion details on the outside back.

of the welt. Tack in place with 4 oz tacks. Cut the cover fabric about two inches over the measurement of the back. Blind tack the fabric along the top of the back.

To blind tack the back easily hold the fabric against the back. Throw the material over to the front of the chair. Now place a tack strip along the top inch of the fabric and tack it right next to the welt using 12 oz tacks about every two inches. Bring the fabric back and it will fold over the tacked strip. Fig. 8–9. This is shown in the circle in the figure.

Bring the fabric down over the cotton and stretch it and tack along the bottom of the back rail. Stretch the fabric as tight as you can. Remember to start from the center and work toward the sides alternating from one side to the other as you place the tacks.

Fold the edges along the right and left sides right next to the welt. Stay tack or pin to keep the folds in place. Finish these two sides by blind sewing to the outside arms or by using a tack strip to give a smooth edge.

FRONT PANELS

Some styles of furniture use panels to finish the front of the arms. They are used mostly on styles that have rounded arms such as round arm Lawsons.

The panels are best made of quarter inch plywood although heavy cardboard or fiberboard may be used. If possible use the old panels for patterns for the new ones. Otherwise a drawing of the arm will have to be made and allowances put in for the material, edge, and border. Keep in mind that there is a definite right and a left panel. The panels are identical except that in one the panel top will curve to the right and the other to the left.

Measure the width and length of the panels allowing $\frac{1}{2}$ inch on all sides for tacking. Cut the material to fit.

Make a layer of cotton the exact size of the panel. Do not allow any to hang over the edge. Tack the cotton to the panel with $2\frac{1}{2}$ oz tacks.

Lay the material over the cotton so that it is even on all sides. Carefully turn the panel over and tack the top of the fabric. Stretch the fabric at the bottom and tack. Then tack the sides making sure to stretch the fabric evenly. Cut the fabric where necessary to make it fit the curves on round arm styles.

Now take some welt and run it all around the edge. Start the welt at the bottom and go all the way around the panel. Cut and join the welt at the bottom. Use small tacks to fasten the welt. The completed panel is fastened to the frame by nails. The panel is centered on the front of the arm (sometimes panels are used on outside backs). Several headless nails about $2\frac{1}{2}$ inches long are driven through the front of the panel into the frame. The nails are driven into the fabric until they make an indentation in it. Then a regulator is used to pull the fabric away from the nail gently. The fabric will slip out from under the nail and there will be no opening showing where the nail is. The headless nail has a tapered end that replaces the head and that will not cut the fabric. When it is driven through the fabric it is invisible. Fig. 8–10.

Where Naugahyde or leather are used nails would leave a mark. Panels upholstered in these types of materials are blind nailed to the frame. This is done by taking a tack strip that will go along the entire

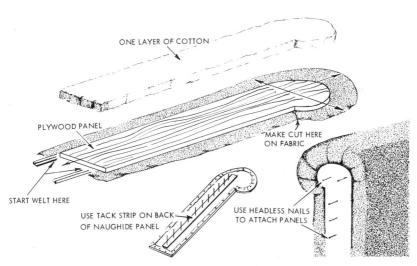

ONE LAYER OF COTTON

PLYWOOD PANEL

MAKE CUT HERE
ON FABRIC

START WELT HERE

USE TACK STRIP ON BACK
OF NAUGHIDE PANEL

USE HEADLESS NAILS
TO ATTACH PANELS

Fig. 8-10.   Making and placing the front panels.

height of the panel. The tack strip is fastened to the panel in the middle of the back by using a strong glue designed for use on paper and wood. When the tack strip has been securely glued to the wood of the panel, the panel is centered on the arm and a rubber mallet is used to drive the tacks into the frame by pounding on the face of the panel. Be sure to pound the panel as the padding will absorb a great deal of the force of the blows. Use a rubber mallet that will not damage the fabric or padding.

Hand made panels are made without using a form. This method takes a little longer and produces a different effect. The entire face of the arm is covered with a layer of cotton. Trim this so it fits exactly and tack in place. Cut a piece of fabric to the exact shape allowing enough to fold under the edges. Fold in the outside edge to the exact shape and stay tack. Be sure that the edges are straight and even. Finish the edges by using decorator tacks or nails. Be sure to keep the decorator nails on a straight line. This can be done by making a chalk line with a ruler. The nails can be spaced by using a small piece of cardboard for measuring the space between them. The decorator nails should be selected to give the best effect on the material you are using.

Another way of finishing the hand made panel is to add welt before putting on the cotton. The cotton is trimmed so that it is about a half inch inside the welt. Then the fabric is applied and blind sewed through the welt and to the inside and outside arm covers.

DECORATIVE NAILS

Some styles of furniture have a wood trim that is not covered by the outside fabric. The edges of the fabric next to the wood are often finished by having decorative nails used along the edge to help hold the fabric and to add an ornamental appearance. Fig. 8–11.

There are several kinds of nails used for this purpose. Some are called metaline and are round head tacks coated with enamel in color to match or contrast with the covering. Other kinds have various shapes of head such as star, fluted, hammered, and round.

The decorative nails can be applied in several ways. One is to have the heads touching so a line of them follows the line of the furniture.

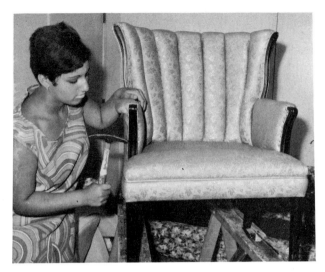

Fig. 8-11. Decorative nails being used to finish an outside arm.

If this style is wanted be sure to mark a line with a piece of sharpened chalk where the nails will go. This will avoid having the nails get out of line.

Often the nails are spaced along the edge. In this case be sure to mark the line and also use a gage for keeping the nails the same distance apart. A gage can be made from a piece of cardboard cut to the width of the space desired. When a nail has been partly driven in place the gage is placed against it and the next nail started at the edge of the gage.

When using decorative nails even spacing is important so even although you are using a gage for spacing and line for having them placed correctly do not drive them all the way in. When there are a number of them partially driven look at the effect from a little distance and notice if they are evenly spaced and following the correct line. Correct any that are not. Then finish driving them in all the way.

APPLYING GIMP

Gimp is a specially manufactured trimming material. It is used as a decoration in some cases and to cover edges in others. Gimp is used mostly on furniture that has exposed wood surfaces where the fabric stops at the edge of a tall leg or a front or side rail. These edges must be tacked and gimp is used to cover the tacks.

There are several patterns in gimp but a scroll type is most popular. Gimp can be used in contrasting colors or it can be matched to the color of the fabric. One firm carries over a hundred colors of gimp.

The simplest way to attach gimp is to merely tack the gimp over the edge of the cover along the wood. Special gimp tacks are used. These are dark blue thin tacks with small, round heads. When they are carefully placed and driven in they are almost invisible. The gimp tacks should be placed near the outside edge of the gimp and staggered to keep the gimp from curling.

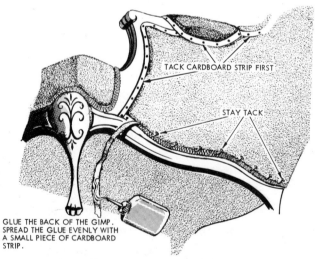

TACK CARDBOARD STRIP FIRST

STAY TACK

GLUE THE BACK OF THE GIMP. SPREAD THE GLUE EVENLY WITH A SMALL PIECE OF CARDBOARD STRIP.

Fig. 8-12. Gimping an antique chair.

Another way is simply to apply glue to the back of the gimp and stick in on the fabric. Stay tack until the glue sets.

What I personally feel is the best way to apply gimp is over a cardboard strip. A strip of cardboard such as a tacking strip is tacked all around the edge. The cardboard is trimmed so that it is about $\frac{1}{16}$ of an inch narrower than the gimp. The gimp is then glued to the cardboard strip and stay tacked until the glue sets.

In gluing gimp use a small brush or a strip of wood or cardboard or an applicator bottle to spread the glue on five or six inches of the gimp. Use a thin layer of good furniture glue. Press the gimp firmly on the cardboard or fabric and use a 4 oz tack about every five inches to hold it in place. Remove the tacks after the glue has dried, about two hours.

The method of using a cardboard strip is a little more work but a smoother, more durable job is the result. Fig. 8–12.

MAKING A FLOUNCE

Some styles of furniture are finished with a fabric skirt that covers the space between the floor and the bottom of the seat. This skirt or flounce is ornamental and may be added or removed according to the taste of the user. There are several styles of flounces; the three most popular are the corner pleated, the box pleated, and the gathered or shirred flounce.

If a flounce is desired it should be fully lined. This will make a tremendous difference in its appearance and also in its durability.

When a flounce is completed and before it is applied to the furniture it should be pressed. This is best if it can be done on a commercial pressing machine. This will set the creases in the pleats and remove wrinkles without creating a shine or a flattened look.

The first step is to measure the height of the flounce. Measure from the very bottom of the leg to about $1\frac{1}{2}$ inches above the top of the leg. This will give allowance for seams and welt.

Now cut the number of pieces of fabric needed for the style of flounce you have selected. Be sure to cut these across the width of the material. Sew the ends together so a long strip about 8 inches high and 15 to 20 feet long is made.

Cut a strip of muslin about an inch narrower in height and the same length. This will be about 7 inches by 15 to 20 feet.

Lay the fabric face down. Now lay the muslin alongside of the fabric and with about a half inch overlapping the fabric. Run a straight seam along this overlap. Next bring the edges of the fabric and the muslin together and run a seam close to the edge. Press to set the fold on the bottom edge and to smooth the flounce.

CORNER PLEATED FLOUNCE

On chairs only one pleat is used at each corner while a sofa will generally have one at each corner and additional ones where the cushions meet. For most furniture this will require $3\frac{1}{2}$ strips of fabric for a chair and 6 strips for a sofa.

To make the pleat start near the center of the lined strip of fabric. Fold half the width of the pleat under the fabric toward the right and then fold the other half underneath toward the left. If you are planning

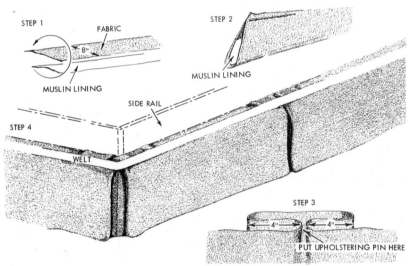

Fig. 8-13.   A corner pleat flounce.

on an 8 inch pleat fold the fabric under to the right for 4 inches. Then go to the left and make another 4 inch fold so the two folds meet in the center of the pleat. Pin these folds in place.

Now measure to the next corner and make a similar pleat. Be sure to start the pleat on the exact distance from the center of the other pleat. Repeat this on all four corners. On the last pleat plan to join the fabric at the back of the pleat so the seam will not show.

When the pleats have all been pinned try the flounce on the chair and check to be sure the center of each pleat comes at the exact corner. If not, then repin and adjust. When the flounce is correctly pinned sew a seam across the top of each pleat to hold it in place. Fig. 8–13.

Next sew a welt all around the top of the flounce. Be sure to start the welt at the part of the flounce that will be on the back side.

BOX PLEATED FLOUNCE

This style will take about $4\frac{1}{2}$ widths of fabric for a chair or about 20 feet when it is sewed together. This flounce is easily made if two pieces of cardboard are cut for patterns. Determine the width of the pleats by measuring the width of the chair front and then divide this width so that some even number is obtained. This will avoid having part of a pleat going around a corner.

Cut a piece of cardboard that is this width and about the height of the flounce. Cut another piece that is just half the width. Choose a point that is somewhere near the middle of the material. Place the wide piece of cardboard underneath the fabric and hold securely. Now take the half piece of cardboard and put it on top of the fabric and slide a fold of the fabric underneath the wide piece of cardboard until the half piece of cardboard is covered by the wide piece. Pin this fold. Remove the cardboards and lay the half width on top of the material and right up against the edge of the fold. Now take the wide cardboard and push a fold of the material over the half piece until the fold meets the first fold. Pin in place. Now take the half cardboard and slide a fold under the other side of the wide piece. Just keep moving the cardboard and sliding them under each other in this way until you have made as many pleats as you will need.

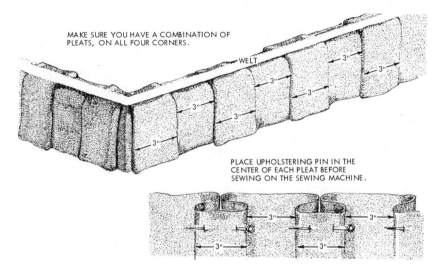

MAKE SURE YOU HAVE A COMBINATION OF PLEATS, ON ALL FOUR CORNERS.

WELT

PLACE UPHOLSTERING PIN IN THE CENTER OF EACH PLEAT BEFORE SEWING ON THE SEWING MACHINE.

Fig. 8-14.   A box pleat flounce.

When all of the pleats have been pinned measure them on the chair. Be sure that the pleats are evenly spaced across the front of the chair. (Note: Most chairs are wider across the front than they are from front to back. Consequently the pleats at the back corners may not come out even with the corners. If there is only an inch or two that goes around the corner the pleats may be adjusted slightly to avoid this by making each pleat along the side slightly narrower. Be careful to keep the appearance uniform.) Join the material at the back of the chair under one of the pleats. Now sew a plain seam all along the top of the flounce to hold the pleats. Sew a welt along the top edge and the flounce is ready to be fastened to the chair. Be sure to start the welt at the back part of the flounce. Fig. 8–14.

GATHERED OR SHIRRED FLOUNCE

This style of flounce is hard to measure as the amount of gathering makes a great deal of difference. However, this flounce will usually take at least $4\frac{1}{2}$ widths of the fabric.

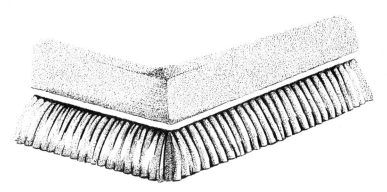

Fig. 8-15.   A gathered or shirred flounce.

To make the shirring, take the lined fabric and run a heavy thread through it about an inch from the upper edge. Make the stitches about the size you wish the folds to be. When the thread is all the way through the fabric fasten the ends so that the flounce is hanging horizontally. Slide the fabric along the thread so that the puckers are about even. Pin several places to keep the material in place and sew the flounce just above the thread. Pull the thread out. Sew on the welt.

When this type of flounce is fastened to the chair it will stick out like an inflated parachute. Push it down and tie down with a piece of twine. Leave the twine on for a few days and the flounce will start to assume its natural position. Fig. 8–15.

TACKING THE FLOUNCE

The chair or sofa is turned upside down for the last operations—tacking the flounce and cambric. The front of the flounce is placed across the front of the chair and stay tacked at each side and about every 7 inches. Measure the proper position of the flounce by adding $\frac{1}{2}$ inch to the height of the flounce. This is the distance that the flounce should be tacked from the bottom of the leg. When the chair is turned upright the flounce will just clear the floor. If deep rugs are used the distance can

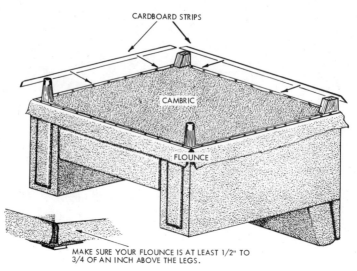

CARDBOARD STRIPS

CAMBRIC

FLOUNCE

MAKE SURE YOUR FLOUNCE IS AT LEAST 1/2" TO
3/4 OF AN INCH ABOVE THE LEGS.

Fig. 8-16. Fastening the flounce to the frame.

be increased to $\frac{3}{4}$ of an inch. When the flounce has been stay tacked hold it up against the legs. There should be $\frac{1}{2}$ inch of the wood showing.

Next take a cardboard strip and lay it along the flounce up against the welt. Tack it every 2 inches with 12 oz tacks. Continue the blind tacking all around the chair. Be sure to keep the cardboard in a straight line and close to the welt. Fig. 8–16.

APPLYING CAMBRIC

This completes the upholstering. While the chair is still upside down place a piece of black cambric over the bottom. About a square yard will do. Be sure the shiny or glazed side of the cambric is facing up. Cut the cambric to fit the bottom allowing about an inch on both width and depth for tacking. Stay tack the cambric. Start at the front and tack from the center to each corner, smoothing the cloth. Now stretch the cambric to the back and tack. Remember that in tacking cambric as with burlap and muslin that about a half inch is folded under for reinforcement when tacking. Fig. 8–16. Turn the chair over and add the cushion and the upholstering is completed.

INSERTING BUTTONS

Placing buttons on a project can make the difference between a completed project or, in some cases, an over-dressed one.

A tufted back definitely requires buttons. Some plain fabrics are improved in appearance by using some buttons, and some styles need buttons to look right.

There are several sizes of buttons and the size selected should be in keeping with the size of the furniture.

Buttons are almost always covered with the material used for the cover. There are machines made to cover buttons easily and rapidly. The hand operated button machines use several dies to make the button. One die is a circular cutter and cuts the cloth the right size. The circle of fabric is placed in a die with a metal inner mold under it. Then a bottom mold which may contain a tuft of cloth, a loop of wire, a nail, or metal prongs is placed on another die and the machine is operated by first pressing down on the first die and then on the second. The molds and dies act together to form the fabric around a circular mold that is curved upward and then to lock the fabric in the mold by inserting the back mold which has the fastening device in it. Fig. 8–22.

Some places may cover buttons with your fabric for a small fee. Ornamental buttons can also be obtained that have a finish that will blend with many kinds of fabrics.

The buttons that are tied on are the most widely used in upholstery as the length of the fastening can be adjusted by merely adjusting the twine holding the buttons in place.

In placing buttons on backs, seats, cushions, and other places first mark the center lines lightly with chalk. Then measure in each direction and mark the places where you want the buttons taking care to keep them uniformly spaced. Mark each place with chalk. In case you are fastening the buttons to the webbing you take a button and thread it with a length of #252 twine about a foot long. This gives you two ends each about 6 inches long. Thread both these through a tufting needle, Fig. 8–23. Push the needle through the center of one of the chalk marks and right on through the back. Pull the twine and tighten the button

Fig. 8-17. A small button covering machine.

Fig. 8-18. Dies on button machine.

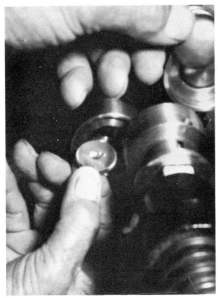 

Fig. 8-19. Inserting button mold in machine.

Fig. 8-20. Completed button in machine.

Fig. 8-21. Dies for cutting button covers.

Fig. 8-22. Cutting button covers with die and mallet.

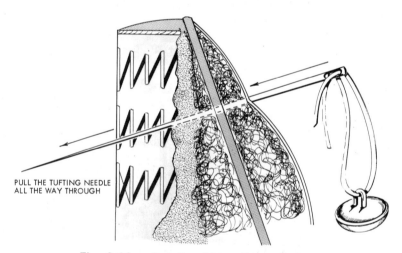

PULL THE TUFTING NEEDLE
ALL THE WAY THROUGH

Fig. 8-23. Details of inserting a button.

against the fabric. Next, make a lock knot in the twine. As you draw up the knot place a small wad of cotton in the loop so that the twine will not pull through the webbing. Tighten the knot until the button forms the desired depression in the fabric. Lock the knot and cut off the ends. Tie one row of buttons at a time starting from one side. Keep checking to see that the indentation made by each button is uniform.

Some cushions, such as pillow type as well as others, have buttons on both sides. In this case both sides of the cushion are marked with the same measurements. The needle is pushed through being careful to see that it comes out through the center of a corresponding mark on the other side. Then a second button is threaded through one end of the twine and a lock knot is made in the twine. The knot is pulled up until the buttons on both sides make about the same indentation. Then the knot is locked and the ends of the twine cut off close to the button and tucked under it.

Buttons used on seats, backs, and cushions are almost always tied in place. On headboards, doors, arms, and other surfaces that have rather thin padding and a wood backing or frame the buttons can be obtained with large tacks or small nails in them that are driven into the wood. In driving a nail type button be sure to use a piece of cloth over it and a rawhide mallet to drive it. This will prevent the fabric covering of the button from being injured by the hammer.

UPHOLSTERED BOTTOM BAND

The front seat of a chair or sofa is a decorative and conspicuous area and can be finished in several ways. One way is to use a flounce, another is to use gimp or other trim, and a third is to upholster a bottom band across the front. This is the one we will discuss here.

An upholstered bottom band is actually a simple process. However, it adds a quality look to the furniture and gives an appearance of luxury.

The first step is to determine the height of the bottom band. Usually a band of 4 inches across the width of the seat is used. The bottom band goes across the width of the chair or sofa just below the front seat. In many styles these both stop at the inside of the front arm. There are some styles, especially those with extended or "T" shaped cushions, where the front seat and the bottom band go back to the arm. These styles may go to either to the inside or the outside of the arm. Be sure to check this before measuring the width of the bottom band.

Measure from the bottom of the front rail and mark off 4 inches (if this is the height you selected) on each side. Tack welt at one of the marks and run it across the front to the other mark and tack it. Be sure to stretch the welt as tight as you can so that it makes a straight line across the chair.

Cut some cover fabric the length of the welt plus an inch, and about 6 inches high (for a 4 inch band). Use cardboard strips and blind tack this right against the welt. Tack about every 2 inches with 12 oz tacks. Throw the tacked piece up over the front seat so it will be out of the way.

Tack another strip of cardboard along the bottom edge of the bottom rail so the cardboard extends or sticks out about ⅟₁₆ of an inch beyond the wood. This will give a sharp edge. Fig. 8–24.

Cut a piece of cotton the width of the band and about twice the height. A 4 in. band would need an 8 in. piece. Fold the cotton double and put the fold next to the welt. Tack in place through the bottom layer of cotton. Use 4 oz tacks. Now bring the fabric over the cotton and to the bottom of the rail. Be sure that the cotton does not hang over the rail

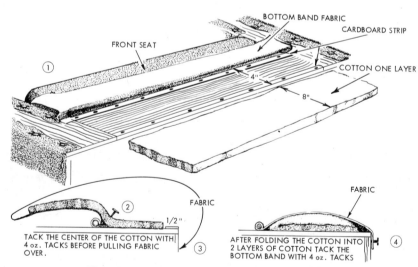

Fig. 8-24.   Upholstering the bottom band.

beyond the bottom edge. Pull the fabric tight at one corner and fold about a half inch back to make a smooth edge along the arm. Tack in place on the bottom rail. This fold can be blind sewed or blind tacked. Do the same at the other corner. Finish by tacking along the bottom of the rail with 4 oz tacks.

UPHOLSTERING AROUND THE LEGS

Finishing the chair or sofa may require some special techniques to provide smooth edges around some styles of legs. Where the legs are set back under the furniture the front arm is finished like the outside arm. The fabric is folded under the frame and tacked. In styles with ornamental wood surfaces around the leg blind tacking may be used or tacking along the edge of the wood and then covering with decorative nails or gimp to conceal the tacks can be done.

Where the legs are at the edge of the frame the problem is to carry the smooth edge of the outside arm and the front seat or bottom band around the leg so that a smooth and finished appearance is obtained.

The method of upholstering around a leg is absolutely the same whether the leg is round or square and whether the furniture is a chair, divan, or sofa.

When you have finished tacking about 90 percent of the outside arm and the part of the fabric that goes on the arm front you are ready to finish the work around the legs. This is shown in Fig. 8–25, in the top sketch. You will notice that the fabric has not been tacked up to the leg on either the outside arm or the arm front.

Cut the fabric with your scissors as shown in the center illustration. Start the cut an inch inside the edge of the leg and complete the cut at the exact point where the leg and frame meet as shown by the arrows. Cut the same on both the front and side of the leg.

Now fold the fabric on the leg up and under the part on the arm. You will need a screw driver or putty knife to push the fabric up under the other part. Be sure the cuts were made the same on each side so you can make a straight fold along the edge of the leg. Push the fabric all the way up to prevent bunching and lumping.

Next take the remaining pieces and fold them so the fold is in a

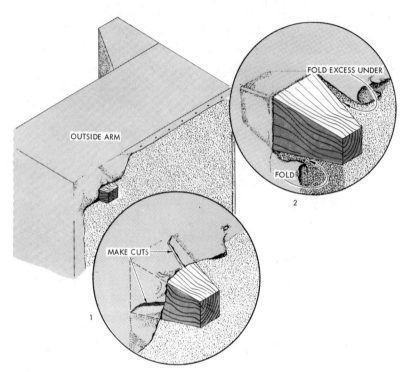

FOLD EXCESS UNDER

OUTSIDE ARM

FOLD

2

MAKE CUTS

1

Fig. 8-25.   Upholstering around legs.

straight line with the corner of the leg and alongside of it. Take the
fold and tack it to the frame very tightly right up to the corner. Do this
on both sides of the leg. This is shown in the lower part of the illustration. If you have made the cuts accurately you will have a fold that
runs along the bottom of the frame and around the leg to the arm front.
The fold is tacked along the bottom of the side arm and the bottom of
the arm front and tucked up under the fabric on the corner of the arm.
Firm tacking is important to prevent the tucked-in part from working
loose.

Where the outside fabric is heavy or where there is a seam and welt
as in the case of the square cover that is made and then pulled over the

arm it may be necessary to cut a slit in the center of the piece over the leg so that the fabric can be pushed up underneath. Be sure that this slit does not come all the way down to the fold.

COVERING WITH PLASTICS

Plastic materials for covering furniture are widely used on some styles. Some of the advantages of plastic coverings, such as Naugahyde are scuff resistance, spot and stain resistance, durability, and special finishes such as imitation leather. While the plastics can be handled like fabric in most cases there are one or two precautions that should be used. One is that they are not as easy to blind sew. It is neater and simpler to blind tack them using cardboard strips and tack strips. The use of tack strips was described in finishing the outside back. Decorative nails can also be used in some styles.

One problem that sometimes arises with plastics is that they wrinkle on curved areas.

For example a curved or round back chair will often wrinkle in the middle of the back. To eliminate this tack the plastic at the top and bottom as tight as possible, then smooth out as much as you possibly can and stay tack along the sides.

To remove any wrinkles take a heat lamp and hold it about 6 inches from the plastic just long enough for the material to heat and soften slightly. Be careful that the material is only heated enough to soften. Too much heat may ruin it. Now work the wrinkles out of the softened plastic to each side and finish tacking. This can also be done by placing the chair in the hot sun for a short time. Be sure not to overheat the plastic or overstretch it when it is hot.

QUESTIONS FOR STUDY

1. What is outsiding?
2. What is meant by blind tacking?
3. Why is blind sewing used on the outside?
4. Why are panels used on some styles of furniture?
5. Name three styles of flounces.
6. Where is a flounce fastened?

7. Should a flounce be lined or unlined? Explain.
8. Where is cambric applied?
9. What is the purpose of the cambric?
10. When is gimp used?
11. What is Naugahyde?
12. Where is it used?
13. What are some of the advantages of plastics?

Chapter 9

Problems
of
Special Styles

Furniture styles change just as clothing, interior decorations, and automobiles do. Furniture styles often reflect periods of history when they originated such as Louis XIV, Louis XV, and Louis XVI styles in France and Queen Anne, Victorian, and William and Mary in England. The Colonial period in this country added several distinctive styles and more have been added in the periods since then. Virtually all of these styles have persisted and are being manufactured today. See Fig. 9–1. Each style has its own group of adherents.

Consequently there are a great many styles and kinds of furniture that are encountered in upholstery work. Often furniture will be kept for generations because of historical or sentimental value. Antiques will be restored to match the decor of some room and other pieces of furniture will be renewed simply because they are comfortable.

As a result the upholstery craftsman must have wide knowledge of most of the basic types and the methods used in repairing and renewing them. Some of the special techniques are covered in this chapter.

Generally these more intricate techniques can be mastered if care and patience are observed. Doing the work first in muslin will provide practice and will help to prevent expensive mistakes when the final fabric is put on.

CHANNEL BACK

Channel back furniture can be exceptionally attractive and distinctive. While there are some people who feel that a channel back is not

Fig. 9-1.   Patterns are used to mark fabric in factories.

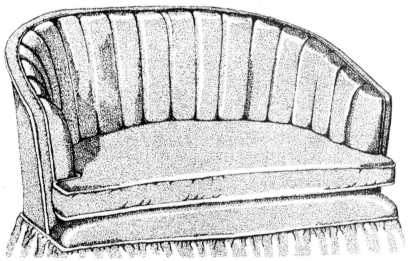

Fig. 9-2.   A channel back chair.

very comfortable, this is often the result of not having proper softness in the upholstering. Fig. 9–2.

In creating a channel back be sure the back springs are tied low and that there is no edge wire. Stretch burlap over the back springs. Apply a layer of cotton over the entire back. Tack in place.

Now measure the width and height of the back. Fig. 9–3. Cut two pieces of muslin the size of these measurements with tacking allowance of about two inches on each dimension.

Tack one of the muslin pieces to the bottom rail. Then pull it as tight as possible and tack across the top of the top rail. Tack the sides firmly to the side rails. Be sure the muslin is quite firm and tight.

Measure the muslin across the back between the arms and then measure the width at the widest point. Find the exact center of the back from these two measurements. Fig. 9–3. Draw a line on the center of the muslin with a pencil or a ball point pen. Be sure to mark the muslin that is fastened on the bottom of the bottom rail and also on the top of the top rail.

Now we have to determine the size of the channels. This is done by dividing the widest part of the back into an even number of parts. Select

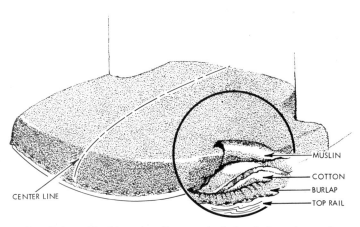

Fig. 9-3.   Marking muslin on chair back for channels.

a figure of the approximate width of the channels you would like to make—3,4,5,8 or 10 inches. Divide this into the width of the back. Try different widths for the channels until you find one that will make an even number of channels in the width of the back such as 6,8,10, 12 or more. In the illustration a figure of 5 inches was found to be right. Regardless of the size of the channels or the piece of furniture the procedures are absolutely the same. Fig. 9–4, top.

On the second piece of the two pieces of muslin that you cut first and that is the same as the one tacked over the cotton, mark off the widths of the channels. Be sure to mark the muslin in the exact center before you start as the channels must be even on both sides of the center. Fig. 9–4, top.

Next plan the layout of the channels on the finish fabric by taking the width of the channels that you want (five inches in the example shown) and adding two inches to each of the inside channels and four inches to each of the outside channels. This makes the inside channels seven inches and the outside channels nine inches. In the illustration there are eight channels of seven inches in width and two of nine inches.

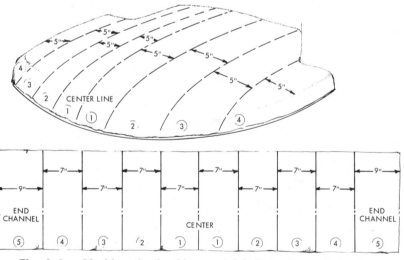

Fig. 9-4.   Marking the backing and fabric to form channels.

This adds up to 74 inches. ($8 \times 7 = 56 : 2 \times 9 = 18 : 56 + 18 = 74$). Fig. 9–4, bottom.

The fabric is only 54 inches wide so 20 inches more are needed. However, the seam must come on one of the lines so a piece at least 23 inches wide must be used. This is obtained by adding the amount of fabric needed for the outside channel and as many inside ones as necessary. In this case the figures are $9 + 7 + 7 = 23$ inches. Add another inch for seams and cut the piece across the width of the fabric 24 inches wide. The height should be the same height as the channels that you measured before. It is necessary to cut across the width of the fabric so the weave and pattern will be running the same way. If there is a large figure or pattern in the fabric be sure to match the two pieces before cutting the additional piece. This may require adding more to the additional piece beside the 24 inches needed. Remember to include enough extra material for tacking on the sides, top and bottom.

When you have cut and joined the fabric to the dimensions you will find that it is considerably wider than the piece of muslin you have marked. This is due to overallowance. This overallowance is necessary to give room to make the channels. The outside material has to be wider to go around the thickness of the padding. It will be padded out in a number of loops.

Take the fabric that you have cut to the dimensions of the back plus the overallowances, and mark the back side with pencil. This will be the layout shown in Fig. 9–4 at the bottom.

Now sew the cover and the marked muslin together. Place the lines on the back of the cover and the lines on the face of the muslin together and sew together with a heavy thread. Sew only the inside lines, leaving the two outside channels open. These will have to be fitted around the arms and must be finished on the chair. When the sewing is finished you will have a number of loops or channels in the finishing fabric. Fig. 9–5.

The next step is filling the channels. This is much simpler if you have a device to put the padding in place. You can make one of metal or construct a simple one of plywood and cloth. To make one of plywood obtain a piece of $\frac{1}{4}$ inch plywood that is about 2 inches narrower than the channel. For a five inch channel use a 3 inch width of plywood about

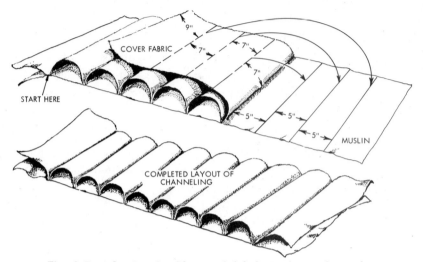

Fig. 9-5. Sewing backing and fabric to form channels.

36 inches long. Sand the plywood smooth and round the edges. Varnish, lacquer, or enamel the plywood so a smooth, glossy surface is obtained.

Now make a sleeve of polished cotton or silk cloth. For a five inch channel use a piece of cloth about 9 inches wide and 45 inches long. Sew this into a long tube.

To fill the channels cut cotton three inches longer than the channels are deep. Roll the cotton into tight rolls the same size as the channels and packed as dense as you would like the channels to be. The tightness of rolling determines the density.

Place the roll of cotton on the plywood. Pull the cloth sleeve on over the plywood and the cotton. Squeeze the cotton into the sleeve or tube.

Now slide the filled tube into a channel. With your left hand grasp the tube, cotton padding, and fabric at the bottom. With your right hand pull the plywood out of the sleeve at the top. Fig. 9–6. Next grasp the cotton padding, bottom muslin, and fabric at the top and then use your other hand to pull the sleeve out at the bottom. This leaves the padding

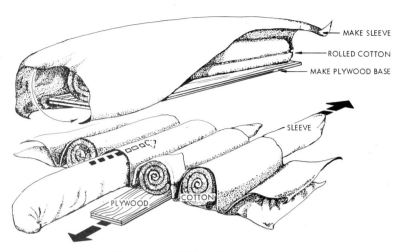

Fig. 9-6.   Filling the channels.

inside the channel. Fig. 9–6. Continue this until all the inside channels
are filled.

Foam padding is used to pad channel back furniture quite often. The
foam is cut the same length as the cotton, that is about three inches longer
than the channel. Foam padding of three inch thickness is used and the
padding is cut the same width as the channel. The three inch thickness
of the foam gives a firm yet soft cushioning.

In filling the channels with foam padding the padding is squeezed
together and pushed into the channel for about halfway. Fig. 9–7. Then
the foam is grasped by reaching in from the other end of the channel
and pulling all the way down to the bottom of the channel. Use the foam
just as it comes in the slab. Foam that has been wrapped with cotton or
Celocot fibers will bunch when being pulled into the channel. The foam
padding can be put in the sleeve and then inserted like cotton but this
is not necessary as the foam will stand the pulling and squeezing necessary to get it in place without wadding or bunching.

Where the channel is extremely long and there will be a great deal

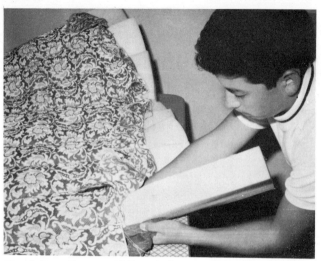

Fig. 9-7.   Foam padding being used to fill channels.

of squeezing at the bottom the padding can be tapered. This is quite easy with foam as the sides can be trimmed with a scissors or knife to the desired shape and this used as a pattern for cutting the rest of the channels.

When all the channels have been filled except the outside ones you lay them in the chair. This is an important and possibly difficult process unless you understand the reasons.

Take the filled channels and place the center of them on the center line of the chair. This is why you were instructed to mark the center line on the top and bottom of the frame when you marked the muslin. Now pull the bottoms of the filled channels down to the bottom rail. This will require a lot of strength to force them in between the seat deck and the bottom rail. The channels are always squeezed together at the bottom and some effort is required to force them in place. When they are pulled down to the bottom rail stay tack with 12 oz tacks. Be sure the center is right on the center line marked on the bottom rail.

Put the chair on the floor and pull the center crease of the channels

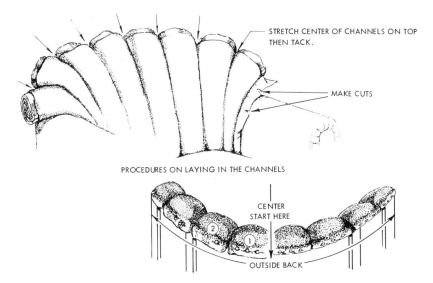

STRETCH CENTER OF CHANNELS ON TOP THEN TACK.

MAKE CUTS

PROCEDURES ON LAYING IN THE CHANNELS

CENTER START HERE

OUTSIDE BACK

Fig. 9-8.   Laying-in the channels in the chair.

as tight as you can. Stay tack it to the center line on the top rail. Work outward from the center pulling each crease between channels as tight as possible and stay tacking it.

This has two purposes. First, it removes any wrinkles that may have formed in the channels, and second, it forces the channels to sink in the center and give a richer, fuller effect. Fig. 9–8.

With the chair at a convenient working height finish off the tops of the channels. Remove any padding that hangs over the back more than three inches. Shove the rest into the channel with your finger tips so that none of it extends over the back of the rail. Pull the fabric in the center of a channel down to the top rail and stay tack in place along the back side of the rail with a 4 oz tack. Then pull outward and down on the fabric at one edge of the channel and tack. Do the other edge. This will produce a rounded, rolled effect. Tack in between the three tacks holding the channel with 12 oz tacks. Do this on all the channels.

Fig. 9-9.   A finished channel back chair.

Now roll two lengths of cotton to fit the outside channels. Cut the fabric at the four points shown on Fig. 9–8, top. Insert the cotton in the channels by hand and push the fabric and padding between the inside arm and the inside back. Tack the fabric to the back of the outside back frame. This completes the back. Fig. 9–9.

Sometimes small buttons may be inserted between channels in one or two places when the channels are very tall.

TUFTED BACK

Tufting is one of the oldest and also one of the most difficult and challenging procedures in upholstering. The Egyptians were the first to use tufting on furniture and were masters of the art using hand made needlepoints and silks and filling them with dried grass. Great amounts of patience and care are required to create a fine piece of tufting. Fig. 9–10.

Fig. 9-10.   A tufted head board.

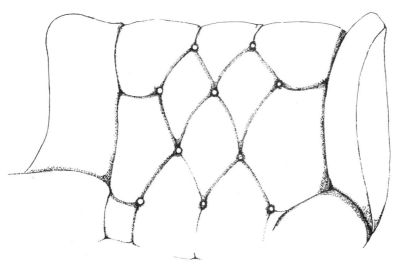

Fig. 9-11.   Diagram of a tufted back chair.

Once the fundamentals are learned the art can be applied to tufting the backs of chairs, sofas, breakfast nooks, headboards, doors and many other upholstered items. Fig. 9–11.

The first requirement is to have a smooth clean surface to work on. Stretch the burlap over the back springs of a chair or sofa quite snug and then cover with a layer of cotton and a muslin cover. Be sure to have the surface smooth and firm.

Be sure the burlap does not pull the springs in. If you pull the burlap too tight you will lose the softness of the springs and the back will be hard.

Now mark the muslin with a pencil or ball point pen on the center lines for both width and height. Make sure the lines are straight and the measurements accurate.

Select the size of the diamond you want. For the illustration a four by seven inch size was selected but any size could be used. The procedure is identical regardless of the size of the diamond or the size of the furniture. Split the diamond over the center point. Fig. 9–12.

Continue to mark off the diamonds as shown in Fig. 9–13. The number of rows of diamonds will depend on the size of them and the height of the sofa or chair. By starting with the center and laying out the diamonds on each side the pattern will come out the same on both sides.

Now count the diamonds that you have across the back and the ones you have from the top to bottom. The figure shows 13 diamonds in the width and two in the height. To the size figure you have selected add an over-allowance on both dimensions of $2\frac{3}{4}$ inches for a shallow tuft and 3 inches for a deep one. So the 4×7 inch tuft becomes a 7×10 when the overallowance is added to make a deep tuft.

The overallowance is necessary to provide enough material to make a pocket in the outside fabric. The same dimensions must be used for marking the tufts and the same overallowance must be made to keep them of the same size.

Multiplying the dimensions (including the overallowance) by the number of diamonds will give the amount of cloth needed for the cover. Thus 13 (number of tufts) multiplied by 7 (width of each tuft after overallowance has been added) gives a total of 91 inches of cloth needed for the cover across the back of the sofa shown.

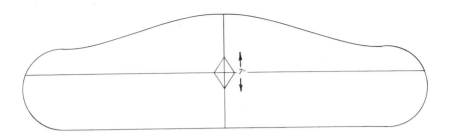

Fig. 9-12.   Laying out a diamond pattern on muslin.

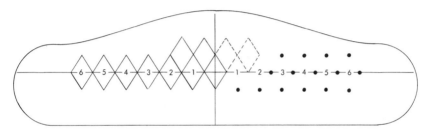

Fig. 9-13.   Marking a sofa to determine diamond pattern.

The fabric comes in 54 inch width so one width will be too small to cover the entire back. Because more than one width will be required it is necessary to splice the cover. While it might be possible to make a straight seam that would not be noticeable in some fabrics, it is better to splice the fabric according to the plan shown. If there is a pattern that needs to be matched then the splicing must be done in such a way that the pattern appears to be continuous all the way across the back and the seams do not show. The same method of splicing would be used if several widths of fabric were needed for a long bench or headboard. The size is immaterial if the idea is understood.

The first step is to cut a width of fabric the height needed. This was found by measuring the back of the chair with the added allowance for the tufts and for tacking. Lay this piece on a flat surface and mark both

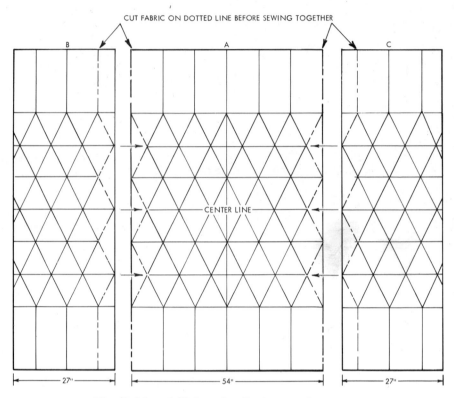

CUT FABRIC ON DOTTED LINE BEFORE SEWING TOGETHER

B   A   C

CENTER LINE

|← 27" →| |← 54" →| |← 27" →|

Fig. 9-14. Splicing details for a tufted back.

the center lines on the back. Then mark out the diamonds using the figures that include the overallowance. When you have done this you will have a piece of fabric marked like the center part of Fig. 9–14.

Count the number of diamonds that you marked on the fabric in both width and height. Find out the number of additional diamonds that you will need by comparing the number marked on the fabric with the number marked on the muslin as shown in Fig. 9–13. Add two inches for tacking at the sides.

If the pattern is repeated in the width of the fabric you may be able to add the necessary amount at one side. However, in large floral designs it may be necessary to add some at each side in order to have a good match of the pattern. Mark each of the side pieces in the same way as the center piece. Then cut off the excess fabric along the diamond pattern as shown by the lines in Fig. 9–14. Be sure to allow about a half inch beyond for a seam. Sew the pieces together using a short stitch and a heavy thread. Check to see that the pattern matches in all the pieces before proceeding. If you cut the center piece first you can lay it face up and then place the side pieces under it at the point where they have been marked. Check to see if the pattern looks right before cutting the side pieces. By cutting along the shape of the diamond the seam will be hidden by the pleat made when the cover is filled.

While it is possible to pad the cover directly many experts feel that muslin should be used and the cover fabric applied over the muslin. The padding can be adjusted under the muslin much easier than under the fabric. Also, it is much simpler to remove the muslin and start over than to try to re-do the tufting with fabric.

One way of marking off the diamonds on a back is to draw in the horizontal lines accurately. Then measure the width of the diamonds working from the center to keep both sides even. Mark the points with a heavy dot. Then draw in the diagonal lines of the diamonds by connecting these points or dots with straight lines. Fig. 9–15.

Take a piece of muslin and make it the size of the cover fabric. That is the full size of the back including overallowance for tufts and backing. Mark this muslin with the size of the tufts including the overallowance for padding. Be sure to work from center lines in laying out the tufts. Fig. 9–16.

Next take a curved needle and thread it with #252 twine. Take the muslin cover that you marked with the oversize diamonds and insert the needle through one of the points of a diamond. Bring the needle back out and pull the twine until about six inches is left hanging. Cut the part attached to the needle about an equal length. This leaves two ends of twine hanging from the stitch, each about six inches long. Continue this until all of the points have been threaded. Fig. 9–16.

Tack this muslin along the bottom rail and at the sides of the first row of diamonds. Take a large straight upholstery needle and thread the two

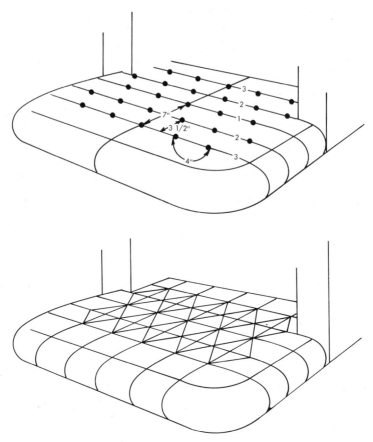

Fig. 9-15.   Marking off diamond points on a chair back.

ends of twine hanging from a diamond point through it. Push the needle
through the point of a diamond marked on the muslin on the chair back.
Be sure that the points of the diamonds correspond in position; that is
that the first point on the cover is threaded through the first point on the
chair back, the second to the second, and so on. The needle is pushed all
the way through the springs and padding and out the back so the twines

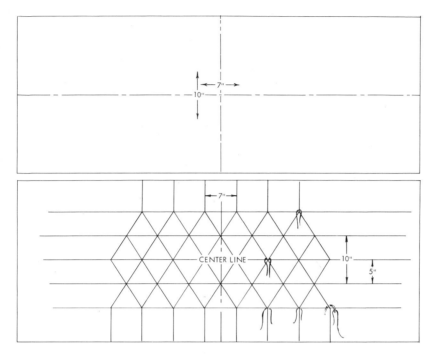

Fig. 9-16.   Marking points on cover. Note threads on points.

are left on the back. Pull the twines so the cover muslin is tight against the other muslin. Make a lock knot in the twine and pull it tight. Be sure to put a small wad of cotton in the loop of the knot before tightening it all the way.

When all of the twines in the bottom row have been tied you will have a number of pouches formed by the two pieces of muslin. Take a small amount of the padding you are using and push it all the way down. Make sure that the points of the diamonds are filled this way. The padding can be dacron fiber, kapoc, cotton, or curled hair. Be sure that curled hair is covered with cotton to prevent the hair from working out. Fill all the pouches with the same amount of padding and check to see if they

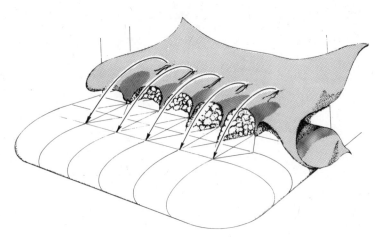

Fig. 9-17. Stuffing the diamonds, first row.

are all about the same size and density. Fig. 9–17. Use a regulator or large needle to move the padding around if it is lumpy.

A beginner will often find that a 70-30 mixture of cotton and curled hair will simplify the work and give a better look to the tufts. Kapoc and Kodel fibers make beautiful tufts but take some practice to handle most effectively.

When all of the pouches in a row have been filled and adjusted tie down the twines in the next row and keep on with the padding. The first attempt frequently does not turn out too well. If the tufts cannot be adjusted by shifting the padding around with a regulator cut the twines at the back of the chair and remove the padding and muslin cover and start over. Fig. 9–18.

When you are padding the tufts remember to check each pocket for density before doing another. The muslin will not make a perfectly shaped diamond because of the lack of body in the cloth. Slight differences in the shape will disappear when the fabric is put on. Try to keep the wrinkles out as much as possible so they will not cause trouble when the fabric is put on.

174   *Upholstery: Refinishing and Restyling*

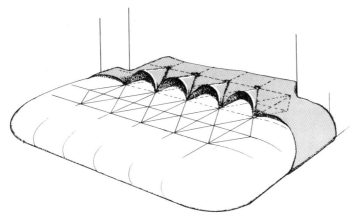

Fig. 9-18.   Stuffing the second and later rows of diamonds.

After the tufting has been completed with the muslin a layer of Dacron or Kodel may be placed over the entire back. Then the finishing fabric is applied over this layer. This is preferable where a very luxurious chair or sofa is desired.

The finishing fabric is marked on the back in the same way as shown in Fig. 9–16. A covered button is threaded with #252 twine and inserted on the outside of the fabric. Be sure the needle comes through the point of the diamond marked on the back. This can be done by using a curved needle and sewing from the back. Leave the twine hang out the back as you did with the muslin. Thread each set of twine through a large needle and push through the point of each diamond where you fastened down the muslin. Pull tight and lock knot as before using a cotton wad under the knot to prevent it from pulling out. Check carefully as you go and make sure that the diamonds are working out uniformly. Adjust with your regulator through the muslin for slight differences.

HEADBOARDS

Diamond pattern tufting is used extensively on headboards (Fig. 9–10) and sometimes on doors and walls. Restaurant booths frequently use this type of upholstering on the backs. Where the headboard or door does not require deep tufting the procedure differs somewhat. A layer of padding, either cotton or foam rubber, is placed over the wooden foundation. The fabric or plastic covering is stretched firmly and tacked at all sides. The cover is marked in the same way as the muslin on the chair back. Chalk is used for making the marks on the cover.

The diamonds are made by using covered buttons with a tack or nail back. The tack is inserted in the center of the mark and driven into the wood. The depth to which the tack is driven will determine the depth of the tuft.

Where a deep tuft is desired foam padding can be slit several inches along the diagonal lines. This will enable the cover to be pulled closer to the wood by the button and will let the foam squeeze up into the tuft. The foam is not cut completely through but only down to the core. It is necessary to mark the foam padding in exactly the same size as the cover for this operation and to see that the slits are the same length and depth on each tuft. Naturally the deeper the padding the deeper the tuft that can be made.

PILLOW BACK CHAIR

The pillow back chair is one of the most comfortable chairs to relax in that can be made. Pillow backs are used on early American, provincial, and English lounge chairs. Figs. 9–19, 9–20.

There are several ways of filling a pillow back. One is to use a back spring unit and cotton. Another is to use a large piece of foam padding about three inches thick and wrapped in two or three layers of dacron. A third way, quite luxurious but expensive, is to use bird down or feathers.

Make the pillow out of muslin and then cover it with fabric. Be sure to use a single piece of fabric for both front and back sides of the pillow. Even if you attach one side of the pillow to the chair there is always a possibility of damage and if that occurs it is a simple matter to loosen the pillow from the chair and reverse it.

The first step after the burlap has been fastened over the springs and padding on the back of the chair is to measure in from the outside of

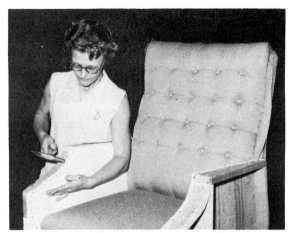

Fig. 9-19.　A pillow back chair.

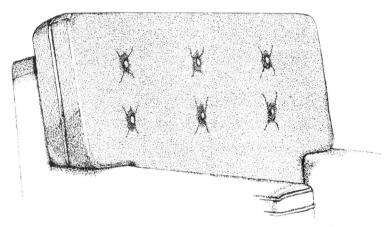

Fig. 9-20.　Detail of a pillow back chair.

the frame a distance of 5 inches on the sides and top. Mark the burlap all around. Fig. 9–21.

Now measure the distance all around the frame and allow enough so that you can sew a 45° angle in the corners. Also allow enough in

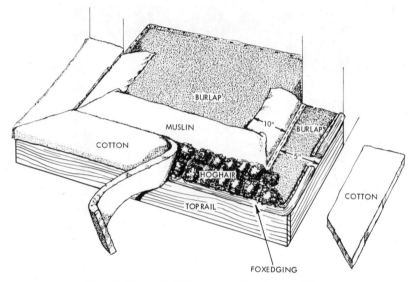

Fig. 9-21.   Building an edge for a pillow.

width so that the material comes over the back of the frame for tacking, about 10 inches. Take some muslin and cut it the size that you have measured. Lay the muslin along the line marked on the burlap and pin it lightly. Fold each corner so a 45° angle is made and pin it. Be sure the muslin hangs over the frame about three or four inches. Remove the muslin and sew the 45° corners, cut off the excess material.

Fasten fox edging all around the outside frame of the sides and back. Allow only a quarter inch of the edging to protrude past the frame. Tack very close to the roll of the edging about every 2 inches with 12 oz tacks. Cut the corners to remove enough material so that a smooth corner can be made. (See Chap. 5, applying fox edging.)

Next, fasten your muslin to the burlap along the line marked on it. Use a curved needle and No. 252 twine. Lay the muslin back on the inside of the back. Fill the area between the muslin and the frame with

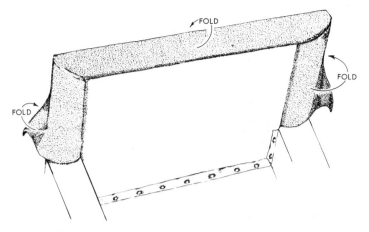

Fig. 9-22.   Finished edge for the pillow.

about ¾ lb. of picked curled hair which should make a pile about 3 inches high and stitch it down as you did when you worked on the arms and backs. Cover the stitched hair with a layer of cotton and bring the cotton out over the frame and the fox edging so that it covers the frame for about an inch. Be sure to make the edge of cotton straight and smooth along the frame. Tack the cotton to the top of the frame. Fig. 9–22. Pull the muslin over the cotton and fasten to the back of the frame. Stay tack the corners first and then stay tack the rest. Finish tacking by starting at the center of the back and work both ways smoothing the muslin snug and wrinklefree. Check the finished roll to be sure it is tight and free from lumps or wrinkles. The muslin will be covered with the fabric when you put the final cover on the back and arms. The roll provides a depression for the pillow to fit into, keeps it snug and prevents it from sliding sideways. Fig. 9–22.

CUTTING OUT THE PILLOW

In making the pillow for the back the first task is to measure the back. Start with the width and measure across the widest part of the

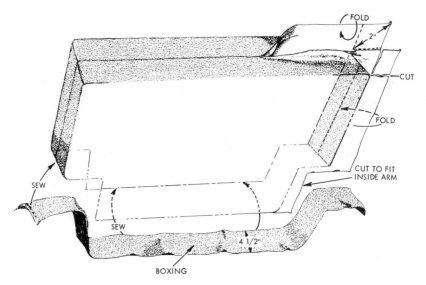

Fig. 9-23. Layout pattern for the pillow.

back and then measure across the highest part of the back. Add two inches on each side so that if your chair is 30 inches wide then allow 34 inches. This extra allowance is for an edge when sewing the two pieces of fabric together. When measuring the height only allow two inches at the top so that a measurement of 35 inches would be increased to 37 inches. Cut two pieces of muslin this size. Remember these figures are only examples, be sure to measure your chair and use those figures.

Cut the muslin to fit the shape of the chair. This is shown in Fig. 9–23. Note that a 2 inch square is cut out at each of the top corners. Also that the part above the arms extends beyond the frame two inches. Now cut the muslin to the shape of the arms with only a seam allowance of a half inch.

Measure the distance around from the top of one arm, across the bottom and up to the top of the other arm. Cut some boxing from the muslin to this length and $4\frac{1}{2}$ inches wide.

When you have cut out all the pieces sew the corners together where you cut out the 2-inch squares. Next sew the two pieces of muslin together along the two inch overallowance. Start at one arm and go up and around to the other arm. This will give a single seam all around both sides and top of the cushion above the arms.

Now sew the boxing to the pillow cushion from one arm to the other and across the bottom. The boxing has to be sewed to both pieces of muslin. However, in sewing the boxing to the second piece of muslin remember to leave the bottom and about five inches on each side open so the cushion can be stuffed. This part of the seam is closed by hand sewing after the filling has been put in place.

While you are doing the pillow in muslin the procedure for the fabric is identical. Follow the instructions and just slip the filled muslin-covered cushion inside the fabric cover. In making the fabric cover welt can be put in from one arm across the bottom to the other arm. The pillow can be finished by placing several buttons in it. Be sure to measure carefully so the buttons are evenly spaced. The buttons can be secured to other buttons on the opposite side of the pillow to make a reversible cushion or they may be fastened to the back of the chair. The pillow is filled in the same way as the other cushions are filled (See Chap. 6). A Marshall unit covered with hair and cotton makes a firm pillow. Foam, either plastic or rubber, will give a soft to firm pillow depending on the density of the material used.

The softest pillows are filled with dacron fibers, kapoc floss, or bird down and feathers. Filling with these loose materials requires more patience and care. Also these pillows should have plenty of buttons to help keep the fibers from shifting and lumping.

Pillows filled with loose material should not be fastened to the back as they will need to be taken off and fluffed occasionally to keep the material in place.

While pillow back chairs are not very common they are found in homes that appreciate comfort and old styles. Even less common are pillow back sofas. However, they do occur and they are upholstered in the same way as the chair. The identical procedures are followed with two or three cushions being used.

OTTOMAN UPHOLSTERING

An ottoman may be used as a footstool or an armless, backless seat. The intended use of an ottoman serves as a guide as to the way in which it should be upholstered. If the use is primarily as a footstool then a simple wooden box with legs and a minimum of padding may serve the purpose. If the ottoman is intended to be used as a seat or in conjunction with a chair as a two piece chaise lounge then the upholstering should be the same as that of the chair. The same procedures are used as you would for a chair seat. The one difference is that a chair seat is finished along the front or front and one or two sides while an ottoman is finished on all four sides.

The ottoman is webbed following the directions for webbing a seat. Springs are fastened to the webbing by sewing. Space the springs about two inches apart each way. This may take more or less springs than a chair seat depending on the size and shape of the ottoman.

Use a sixteen way tie to fasten the springs to the frame. Add an edge wire and cover with burlap. Apply fox edging all around the edge wire.

Cover the burlap with a layer of rubberized hair one inch thick and sew them together. Then add three inches of curled hair, picked fine, on top of the rubberized hair. Sew in place. Place two layers of cotton on top of the hair. Cover with muslin and tack to the frame.

The finishing fabric is cut to cover the muslin and about half or more of the frame. The fabric is tacked along the lower half of the frame if a bottom band is used. Stay tack each corner and then carefully smooth the fabric from the center to the corners and tack every few inches with 12 oz tacks. Cut or fold the corners so that a smooth edge is made. Tack in place. The fabric can be cut large enough to go to the bottom of the frame. It is then tacked to the bottom edge of the rail.

If the ottoman is designed to match other furniture then it should be finished in the same way. If a bottom band is used then the same width band should be used on the ottoman. Other details such as the use of gimp, or decorative nails should be followed.

If a bottom band is used measure the width of the band on the side of the frame. Tack welt along this line. Then blind tack the finish fabric just below the welt. A layer of cotton is tacked on to cover the area from the welt to the bottom of the frame. Bring the fabric over the cotton and tack to the bottom of the rail. More or less padding can be used to match the construction of the other furniture. In cutting the bottom band for an ottoman it is simpler to use two pieces of fabric and have a seam in the center of two sides than to use four pieces and have seams at each corner.

Small size ottomans designed as foot rests may be upholstered with a padding of foam rubber covered by the fabric. This would also be necessary if the frame has a solid bottom instead of an open one.

THE BED DIVAN OR SOFA

Divans or sofas designed to be used as beds are the bulkiest and heaviest pieces of furniture in the home. They are also the easiest to upholster.

There are several styles of bed divans. In some the back folds down to form a bed. In others the seat comes up and out to unfold a cot type spring. In others the bed section slides out.

In any case there are no coil springs in the seat, the problems of webbing, tieing, and other details of installing springs here are eliminated.

The type of bed and the style of the furniture have a bearing on the amount of work needed. In general the springs on a bed sofa are the metal mesh type. These have a mesh of metal strips or wires that are fastened to the frame by small coil springs along the edges. This type of spring is used on some chaise lounges, cots, and similar items. Repair of these springs consists in replacing any broken wires or strips in the mesh and of the small springs that are sagging or broken. Some styles use a No-Snag or sinuous (zig-zag) wire spring. These may need replacing of the stabilizing cross-ties.

In stripping a bed type sofa watch the type of construction all the way through. This will help later when you are replacing the padding and covers.

The instructions that follow are for a style of divan that has a back that folds down to form the bed. The upholstery is termed a waterfall style because the back rolls down to the seat and then to the floor in

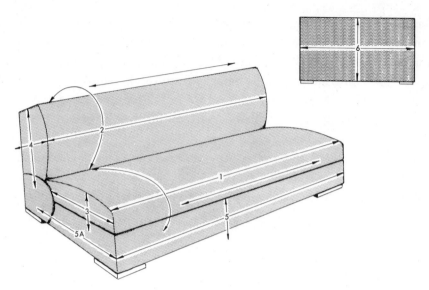

Fig. 9-24.   Upholstering a bed divan.

easy curves. This style has the advantage of being easy to work with and it also eliminates four large seams that are needed with other styles of cover. These large seams are very often the cause of trouble by splitting apart. Because the fabric runs the width of the seat and back a large pattern or one that runs the vertical weave of the cloth would not be suitable for this style. Fig. 9–24.

Bed divans of this type are usually fastened to the base by a few nails or screws that hold the hinges in place. Removing these makes it quite simple to remove the entire seat and back out of the box-like base. It is necessary to remove the bed from the base if there are arms as it is impossible to upholster the ends of the seat and back and the inside arms while the sofa is completely assembled. The armless styles can be upholstered while assembled.

Bed divans of this style can be changed from armless to ones with arms or vice versa with little difficulty. Most arms are held in place by three bolts to the frame. New arms can be attached in the same way.

New arms can be made to order or sometimes obtained ready-made from a frame shop. Several styles of arms can be used and will look well on this piece of furniture.

In upholstering the first operation is to remove all of the old material. When you have done this inspect the springs and make sure that they are straight and have good resilience—bounce. If the springs have lost their shape remove them and replace with new ones. Perhaps the entire spring unit may need to be removed.

When the springs have been checked and repaired or replaced cover them with burlap. Tack the burlap to the frame and stitch to the springs. This is the same operation that is done on the seat of any chair or sofa. Here it is done to both the seat and the back. Now cover the burlap with a sheet of rubberized hair the size of the frame. Stitch all the way around the edge with a curved needle and #252 twine. You can use a large stitch for this.

Next take about $2\frac{1}{2}$ lbs of curled hair and pick it very fine and distribute it over the seat. Do the same for the back. Stitch the hair to the rubberized hair just as you did in upholstering the seat or back of a chair. Use a block stitch.

Now add two layers of cotton over the whole seat and 1 layer over the back. Cover the cotton with heavy muslin. Obtain the 46 inch width and cut it down the middle. You will need about $5\frac{1}{2}$ yards.

Measure the seat and back. Notice that they both go from the place where they meet at the back to the bottom of the spring at the front or at the top. Also measure the end pieces that are needed to form the cover. The seat cover consists of the pieces numbered 1 and 3 while the back cover consists of the pieces numbered 2 and 4. Number 5 is a bottom band. This band will go all the way around in armless styles and will include piece 5A. In sofas with arms only the band across the front will be needed. Fig. 9–24.

In making the muslin cover and the final cover measure the two lines shown at 1 and cut the muslin to fit. Be sure that the muslin reaches the frame at the back and the front. Measure the area marked 3 and make two pieces of muslin this size. Allow for seams. Sew the two #3 pieces to the #1. This makes the seat cover.

Next do the same for the back, measuring areas 2 and 4. Be sure to make two #4 pieces. Sew these together to form the back cover. Turn the covers inside out when you have sewn all the pieces togther so the raw seams will be on the inside. Place the cover over the cotton and stay tack at the four corners.

Then start at the center of the front seat and smooth out the lumps and unevenness. Stretch the muslin by pulling up and toward you. When the muslin is smooth and wrinkle-free tack it to the frame. Keep working from the center toward each end tacking as you go. Smooth and tack the ends. Then work along the last side pulling the muslin down. Be careful not to tack through a place where you are pulling on the muslin. This will leave tack pulls in the muslin.

If the sofa has arms upholster them in the same way as you would a square arm Lawson or whatever style you have. There is no difference.

The bottom band, area #5, is upholstered in the same way as the bottom band on a chair or sofa. In armless styles the bottom band will include area #5A on both ends as well as the front. You can add a flounce if you wish. The procedure is the same as described previously.

Putting the final fabric on the bed divan has one variation from the muslin cover. The fabric is cut the same for the end pieces, #3 and #4. The fabric for the seat and back is cut narrower. It is cut to go from the front frame to the place where the seat and back meet. The fabric should go beyond enough so that no seam is visible. Denim about 12 inches wide is sewed to the fabric along the back edge of the seat or the bottom edge of the back. These are called stretchers and are used to fasten the fabric to the back frames. Be sure to double or triple stitch this seam as it gets a great amount of strain.

Place the fabric cover, be sure the seams are on the inside, over the muslin after you have placed a layer of cotton on it. Tack to the frame in the same way as you did the muslin cover. Be sure to finish tacking the stretcher strips last.

The back, #6, is finished in the same way as the back of a chair or sofa. Refresh your memory by referring to the instructions given on that operation.

In some styles of sofa beds the bottom opens and pulls out to show a folding cot spring. The back and arms remain in place and are upholstered in the same way as you would any sofa. The back may have coil springs. The seat will have two or three removable cushions. Be sure to notice if the cushions are all the same or if there are definite left and right hand ones. A part of the springs of the bed will be padded to serve as a base for the cushions. This padding will have burlap directly over the springs then hair and cotton padding as described. The cover will be similar to that for a chair. That is there will be a front seat of fabric that covers the seat deck for about five inches as well as the front and the back part will be denim. This should be over a muslin cover for best results.

CUSTOM FITTING

Custom fitting a chair to a personal size is not a new art. Many Egyptian and Greek rulers had their personal settees, chaise lounges, boudoir chairs, and other furniture constructed to their personal specifications.

While some people seem to think that having a personal size of furniture is snobbish and conceited, actually the individualizing of a chair for a very tall, a very short, or a very heavy person improves his comfort and may have a bearing on health. Many people who do not fall into the average size range put up with a great amount of discomfort with standardized furniture.

Constructing a chair to an individual size does involve more expense as the frame has to be made by hand instead of being mass produced and different sizes of seat and back springs may be required. However, the difference in cost is not so great when the great improvement in comfort is considered.

The most important part of a custom chair is in having a frame the right size. This means that one should be made to the personal measurements of the user. Once the frame has been made the upholstering follows the identical instructions for a standard size except for the seat springs.

To obtain a frame that will be the right size the person who will use the chair should be measured. This can be done by having him sit in a wooden or hard chair in as nearly a comfortable position as possible and then taking the measurements with a yard stick. A yard stick or a piece of thin board that can be marked is better than using a ruler as there is less possibility of making a mistake or obtaining an incorrect reading. Fig. 9–25.

The first reading is made from the top of the back of the neck down to the seat. This is No. 1 on the drawing. The second measurement, No. 2, determines the comfort of a chair. This is made from the back of the leg calf to the back of the buttocks.

Measurement No. 3 is one that is needed for comfort and health. This is obtained by dropping a yard stick or a board from the back of the shoulders to the seat, keeping the yard stick perfectly upright. Measure the distance to the small of the back.

The next point to be measured is one that is extremely important to a person who has long legs or who has short legs. The yard stick is placed at the back of the leg with the foot flat on the floor. The reading is taken at the back of the knee to give the figure for No. 4.

In measuring for No. 5 you should make an allowance for comfort. This area requires room for relaxing and moving about. There is also a tendency for a relaxed person to slump and the shoulders will spread out so if you have an actual measure of 22 inches across the shoulders when the subject is sitting in a chair, add about 8 inches to give a reading of 30 inches. Add about one-third to the actual figure.

An allowance is also made in determining the width of the seat. For No. 6 you should add about a fifth to the actual measure. If you have a reading of 20 inches add about 4 inches to give 24 inches for the measurement. This is one of the comfort areas and should be ample without being too large.

Dimension No. 7 is often overlooked as a source of discomfort. Unless this part of the chair back is made to fit the individual the shoulders or head may be in an awkward position that will cause muscle strain over a period of time. When sitting in this position the shoulders should be relaxed and the head supported naturally.

Use pillows to support the arm in a comfortable position before making measurement No. 8. Measure from the back of the elbow to the fingertips.

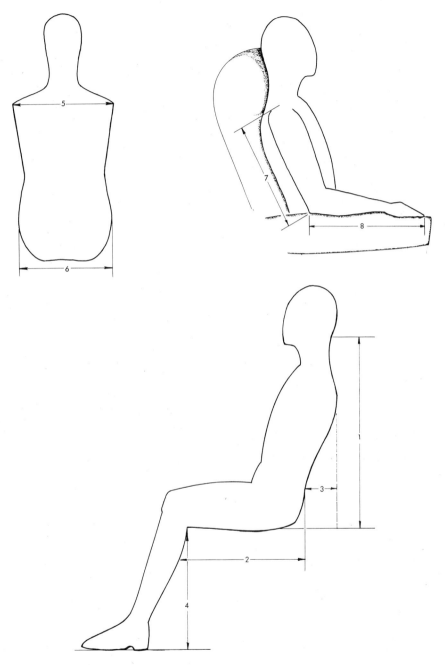

Fig. 9-25. Measuring diagram for a custom frame.

When you have all of these figures make a sketch or tracing of Fig. 9–25 and take it to a frame maker. Mark the dimensions in on the sketch. This will avoid mistakes or misinterpretation. Also find out the weight of the person who is going to use the chair. This may not be necessary for most people but for a very large or stout individual it may be a good practice to use heavier materials as they will give longer service and more comfort. If the person complains of standard seats being too soft or sagging too much, or if the back does not give good support heavier springs may be required.

Occasionally an extremely heavy person will need a much heavier frame. In one case a 325 lb person was fitted for a chair. The frame was made of 2 inch thick stock instead of $1\frac{1}{4}$. The webbing was doubled and the springs were doubled by intertwining them and fastening together with edge wire clips. Tie twines were doubled. The man said that this was the first genuinely comfortable chair he had ever sat in.

The procedure of upholstering a custom frame is identical with that of a standard frame. The only difference comes in selecting springs and adding reinforcement for extremely heavy persons.

QUESTIONS FOR STUDY

1. What is the first step in channeling and tufting?
2. How are the channels created in the fabric?
3. What are overallowances?
4. What is the average overallowance for a channel?
5. How are channels filled?
6. Describe the process of filling a diamond tuft.
7. Name materials used in filling channels.
8. What materials are used for filling tufts?
9. What precaution should be used in filling tufts?
10. How does a pillow back differ from other styles of chairs?
11. Is a sofa bed hard to upholster? Why?
12. When should a custom frame be recommended?

Upholstering as a Business

Upholstering is a skilled craft or profession. It is one of great antiquity and traces its beginnings back to ancient civilizations such as Egypt and even earlier times.

The earliest pictures show evidences that furniture, at least in the palaces, was padded and covered with choice skins or fabrics. Just where or how these upholstered chairs, stools, and couches were made is not known. Probably they were built by skilled craftsmen in the royal courts who learned the trade from some sort of apprenticeship or as a family trade.

The materials that were used by the early craftsmen were the common ones that were available. Weaving is an ancient art and the upholsterers made use of fine fabrics for covering the furniture. Skins of animals were used and still are. Padding consisted of hay, plant fibers, feathers, and bird down, and almost any material that was soft and springy.

While the early business of upholstering was a skilled, individual trade, today it is an important and useful craft with opportunities for many employes in factories and shops.

Upholstering, in spite of the use of modern equipment and materials, is still a hand craft. Skill and training are needed to produce quality furniture as each piece must be specially fitted and adjusted to produce the best results.

There are two large fields of opportunity in upholstering—production upholstering and custom upholstering.

PRODUCTION UPHOLSTERING

This is work performed in a factory and provides opportunities in several categories. There are also opportunities for supervisory and executive positions in connection with the operation of the plant.

The word "production" in connection with jobs often brings to mind assembly lines and numerous workers each intent upon just one operation. In the upholstery field there is no rigidity of an assembly line. Each individual performs many operations in his work. Skill and judgment are needed and there is freedom to do the job. Most operations are done by an individual but there are some instances where small groups of craftsmen work together.

Modern furniture factories work with unions to divide the operations into a number of jobs so that the craftsman can develop proficiency in his own job. Each piece of upholstered furniture is a result of many craftsmen each applying his special skills to produce the best possible result.

Many modern furniture factories are completely self-sufficient. Lumber, fabrics, padding, and other materials come to the factory and are converted into handsome furniture. Generally, the factory is divided into a frame shop where lumber is made into chairs, sofas, and other items and skilled frame makers perform the work, and the upholstery shop were the finished frames are converted into luxurious furniture. For our purposes only the work performed after the frame is completed will be considered as part of the craft of upholstering. Fig. 10–1.

Factories in many areas have set up training programs in cooperation with local schools, federal manpower projects, and unions to teach the trade to prospective employes and to enable the worker to advance in his field.

One of these programs breaks the field of production upholstering into eight major specialties. Each of these requires at least 12 months of actual experience as well as class work to train an apprentice into a journeyman. Some classifications require 18 months where the work is more complex.

Each classification requires some knowledge of all the other ones.

Fig. 10-1.   Frame makers build frames for the upholsterers.

Each must be performed so that subsequent operations will fit in and produce a completed item. Each craftsman must complete his operations in such a manner that the following operations can carry on with no lost time or difficulties.

The furniture industry is composed of more than 3400 factories that do about $4 billion of business a year. One company has 3500 upholsterers working in ten plants and is constantly seeking more employes. This company, as many others, operates a training program for apprentices and pays them a salary during the period of training. Most upholsterers (up to 80% in one plant) work on an incentive plan that rewards proficiency and skill. In order to enable an employe to develop his skills the company divides the various activities into specific operations. For instance, the operation of sewing the fabric is divided so that each seamstress works on just one unit of the chair such as a cushion. In this way skill can be developed in sewing the covers, welt, and boxing together and in installing zippers.

The classification of the various jobs may vary somewhat from plant to plant or in various parts of the country. Basically they are the same. There are eight major job titles with some being further subdivided.

Springer. Obviously the springer installs springs. However, there are several types of springs and this job title is divided into two or three parts. One is a *No-sag springer.* This involves marking the frame for spacing of the springs, fastening the clips to the frame, stretching in the spring, and then fastening the springs with helical springs, or ties, to each other and to the frame. The other kinds of springs are more exacting as the springer must adjust each spring for proper tension and placement. In some places a *Drop-in springer* places the units in the frame, ties the tops of the springs with metal or twine ties, and then covers them with burlap. The *hand tie springer* installs webbing of either jute or metal, fastens the springs to the webbing after determining the proper placing of them, and then ties the springs so that each spring has the required tension, freedom of movement, and correct placement. The tieing of the springs may be done by hand with twine or flexible metal may be used with special clips to fasten it. In either case judgment must be exercised to ensure that each spring works in complete harmony with the others. In some shops the Drop-in and hand tie springs are classified together as both involve skill in tieing and differ mainly in the method of placing the springs in the frame. The springer also covers the springs with burlap.

Seat maker. This job starts with the completed springs. The seat maker adds fox edging (this may be done by the springer) and then adds the filling or padding to the seat and covers it with the final fabric. The seat maker also finishes the front seat area and the bottom band.

Arm maker. This operation takes the project with the seat installed and finishes the inside and top of the arms. This involves putting on webbing and burlap to cover the open areas, adding the filling and padding, and covering with the finishing fabric.

Back maker. He starts with the back springs in place and covered with burlap. He may install edging or welting along the top as needed, puts filling and padding over the springs and then covers with fabric. The back maker also has responsibility for stuffing channels and inserting buttons where the style calls for them.

Outsider. This is listed as *finisher* in some shops. The work is to complete the chair or sofa. As the seats, backs, and arms have been completed only the outside surfaces are left. This requires placing webbing and burlap or cardboard to close the openings in the frame, adding the filling or padding, and covering the entire outside with fabric. This involves blind sewing or blind tacking the visible areas together, and also putting on the flounce if it is used. The final task is to close the bottom of the frame with cambric.

Cushion filler. This is also called cushion *stuffer.* The operations vary depending on the type of cushion being used. It may be a relatively simple job of folding a rubber or plastic foam filler and stuffing it into the cover and closing the zipper. With spring filled cushions the work would require measuring the cover for the spring unit, placing the padding and stuffing around the cushion spring unit, compressing the filling in a cushion filling machine and then putting on the cover.

Cutter. The cutter measures out the fabric on a table. He lays out the pattern on the fabric and marks the fabric. Then he cuts the fabric. This is done on a pile of several layers of fabric and usually electric shears or cutters are used. The cutter assembles the pieces into bundles for sewing. The cutter has to be familiar with the various styles or sizes of furniture and also to use judgment in laying out the pattern to avoid as much waste as possible.

Seamstress. This is listed as a *sewer* in some plants. There are two broad groups, the plain machine sewer and the quilting sewer. The plain machine or seam sewer may be divided into several subgroups such as cushion sewer, flounce sewer, arm sewer, and so on. This enables each person to develop speed and skill on a few kinds of sewing and so increases the opportunity for more earnings under the incentive systems. The quilting sewer does special kinds of sewing and must be highly skilled in sewing designs either from patterns or freehand.

Each plant will have foremen and supervisors so there is often a chance for advancement.

CUSTOM UPHOLSTERING

One classified phone book lists 450 upholstery shops in an urban area. These shops range from neighborhood ones with only the owner doing the work to some large ones that have many employes. Some of these are connected with or operated by department and furniture stores that sell new furniture and that also will renew, repair, or reupholster furniture.

The custom upholsterer is often called a reupholsterer as he almost always works with a used frame and merely adds new upholstering materials to it. However, there is a field for making specialized furniture to order. Fig. 10–2.

The custom upholstering field has several advantages that appeal to many people. There may be no set time or routine other than that dictated by business methods. If the shop is located in or near his home the

Duo-Fast Fastener Corp.

Fig. 10-2. Craftsmen in a large custom upholstery shop.

owner may not need to have any definite hours of operation. Otherwise there should be someone present during normal business hours in the community to take orders, answer inquiries, and handle the customer end of the shop.

The reupholsterer can exercise creative talents in designing new treatments of older styles, and in customizing furniture to special situations. There is no monotony as he must perform all of the operations required. Antiques may provide challenge and problems.

There are some disadvantages as well. The custom shop must perform the stripping operations, repair frames, and do everything necessary to get the frame ready for the upholstery. The shop owner also finds that he must be a businessman as well as a craftsman. He must keep books, advertise and sell his services, pay help, buy materials and supplies, schedule his work load, and be aware of the various laws and regulations that apply to all businesses and also the ones that apply to his only.

Some states and cities have sanitary laws that apply to new or used furniture especially upholstered kinds. Licenses may be required on either a state or local basis. Retail stores usually need a permit of some kind and the definition of what constitutes retail trade should be understood. Building and zoning codes may limit or restrict the location and construction of a shop. Where employes are needed there may be labor laws on wages, hours, working conditions, minimum age, and similar points.

A course in operating a small business would be very helpful and if such a course is not available at some nearby school then a correspondence course should be considered.

In many places there are business services available that keep the books and records, send in tax and other forms, and that handle many of the routine details of office management. These services either pick up the records such as invoices, canceled checks, and correspondence or they may have traveling offices in station wagons or small trucks that come to the business and do the work right there. These traveling offices have adding machines, check writers, typewriters, and various machines that simplify record keeping. The employes handle many kinds of business information and their wide experience enables them to become well acquainted with business methods and laws. Their advice should be extremely helpful in this part of the operation.

In setting up a shop the nature of the work should be kept in mind. Will the shop be only a reupholstering operation that reupholsters furniture on order or will the shop sell new and reupholstered furniture too? There are different regulations that apply in each case. Many states have laws requiring the labeling of bedding and furniture that is sold and sanitary requirements that must be observed. If the work is done on order for a customer there are different rules.

The nature of the work will also be a factor in locating the shop. Where the furniture is picked up, upholstered and returned, the location can be any place where local zoning codes permit it. If furniture is to be sold then a location where there is a flow of people will be needed.

The matter of equipment and supplies must be considered in setting up a custom shop. The first thing is to locate an upholstery supply house or some source of twine, springs, fabrics, padding, burlap, gimp, tacks, staples, and small tools such as stretchers, pliers, clamps, hammers, shears, staplers, needles, and pins. These items will be needed often and should be obtainable without long delay.

Major equipment for a shop would include a large cutting table, trestles, a commercial sewing machine with attachments for making welting, shirring, and other special stitches, a cushion stuffer, either manual or power depending on the size of the business, a button covering machine in a model to handle the expected work, a power stapler for fastening materials to the frame, an electric drill, and an assortment of tools, either hand or power, for sawing, sanding, planing, wire cutting, and painting.

QUESTIONS FOR STUDY

1. How does upholstery differ between ancient and modern times?
2. What major fields of opportunity are there in upholstering?
3. How many classifications of springer are there?
4. Define an "outsider." What else is this job called?

5. Which is more specialized, the factory upholsterer or the shop upholsterer? Why?
6. Name three business problems that the shop operator must know about.
7. List six items of supplies and three pieces of equipment that are needed to set up a shop.

INDEX

Numerals which are in **bold face** indicate illustrations.